LEGAL PATH SERIES®

CIVIL PROCEDURE

Keyed To

Yeazell
7th Edition

ALSO AVAILABLE IN THIS SERIES:

Civil Procedure keyed to: Friedenthal, 10th Ed
Civil Procedure keyed to: Yeazell, 7th Ed
Civil Procedure keyed to: Hazard, 9th Ed
Contracts keyed to: Farnsworth, 7th Ed
Criminal Law keyed to: Kadish, 8th Ed
Criminal Law keyed to: Dressler, 4th Ed
Criminal Procedure keyed to: Kamisar, 12th Ed
Criminal Procedure keyed to: Saltzburg, 8th
Criminal Procedure keyed to: Dressler, 3rd Ed
Constitutional Law keyed to: Chemerinsky, 2nd Ed
Constitutional Law keyed to: Stone, 5th Ed
Constitutional Law keyed to: Sullivan, 16th Ed
Corporations keyed to: Hamilton, 10th Ed
Corporations keyed to: Eisenberg, 9th Ed
Evidence keyed to: Mueller, 6th Ed
Evidence keyed to: Waltz & Park, 10th Ed
Property keyed to: Dukeminier, 6th Ed
Torts keyed to Epstein, 9th Ed
Torts keyed to Prosser, 11th Ed
Torts keyed to Vetri, 3rd Ed

LEGAL PATH SERIES®

CIVIL PROCEDURE

Second Edition

Denise E. Esmerado, Esq.
Seton Hall University School of Law

Mclaren Legal Publishers LLC
New York

ISBN-10: 0-9820734-1-0
ISBN-13: 978-0-9820734-1-4

Published by
McLaren Legal Publishers LLC
552 Broadway, 3rd Floor
New York, NY 10012

www.mclarenpublishing.com
Email: contact@mclarenpublishing.com

Printed in the United States of America

HOW TO USE THIS BOOK

This law school study aid is a "keyed" book. It summarizes all of the major cases in the text book to which it is written and in the order those cases are presented. Our cases are presented in the IRAC format (Issue, Rule, Analysis and Conclusion). Each case uses a text symbol preceding the Issue, Rule, Analysis and Conclusion of the case referenced.

"Repetition is the Mother of Learning"

Throughout each case, many of the key Black Letter law and/or Issues are repeated. You may see the same legal conclusion repeated in the Issue, Rule, Analysis and/or Conclusion. This was done intentionally. All too often, the most important concepts in law school are mentioned only once by a law professor in a lecture hall. However, more often than not, what is mentioned the least is what is tested the most. We feel the more you see (and read) exactly what is important, the more likely you will be to remember it. Recalling key legal points quickly is the key to the successful application of those same rules on an exam. This *is* the difference between an "A" and a "C" for the course.

"All of what you need, none of what you don't"

Our law school study guides give you exactly what you need to understand the key principles of the case, including the sometimes elusive Black Letter law. We are not a replacement for an in depth legal analysis of the subject matter covered; however, we do present what is absolutely critical in a very concise format.

"Do it right in the beginning; it'll be easier in the end"

You may notice that the issues for each case are very specific. They are presented to you as accurately as we can print them. However, be mindful that there may be slight variations in their interpretation from lecture hall to lecture hall. With that in mind, our experience has taught us that if you do the labor-intensive, hard work in the beginning of the course and parse out the specific issue(s), rule(s) and conclusion, the analysis will be easier to formulate and write. It is the analysis of a case that separates the A, B and C grades on an exam (trust me).

"Who's the Plaintiff, who's the Defendant?"

You may notice that in some cases, a case title lists the plaintiff v. defendant in one order but the facts list the parties in the opposite order or may refer to the plaintiff/defendant as the petitioner/respondent/appellant/appellee. This is usually seen, for example, when one party is appealing to a higher court or where various counterclaims and cross-claims are asserted by the parties. When you see the parties change in the facts, keep the procedural history (and the parties) of the case organized in your mind and don't get confused.

Abbreviations used in this book

I This symbol "I" stands for "Issue" using the IRAC method of case analysis. What follows is the issue of the case.

R This symbol "R" stands for "Rule" using the IRAC method of case analysis. What follows is the rule or black letter law of the case.

A This symbol "A" stands for "Analysis" using the IRAC method of case analysis. What follows is the Analysis of the case.

C This symbol "C" stands for "Conclusion" using the IRAC method of case analysis. What follows is the conclusion of the case.

* The Federal Rules of Civil Procedure are often referenced throughout the book as "Federal Rule", "Rule" or "FRCP" followed by the Rule number.

* Use of the word "his" in this book is gender neutral and is meant to encompass both "his" and "her."

ALPHABETICAL TABLE OF CASES

Hawkins v. Masters Farms Inc.

2003 WL 21555767 (D. Kansas 2003)

FACTS

In December 2000, James Patrick Creal was killed when his Chevrolet collided with a New Holland tractor driven by defendant Masters, a Kansas citizen and representative of Master Farms, Inc. (defendant). Plaintiff Mary Ann Hawkins, on behalf of the decedent's estate, sued the defendants in federal court arguing that their negligence was the proximate cause of James's death. In response, defendants filed a motion to dismiss under Federal Rule of Civil Procedure 12(b)(1), arguing that the complaint failed to establish complete diversity as required to confer jurisdiction upon the court. Creal met his wife in 1999 in St. Joseph, Missouri, where he lived with his mother since a prior divorce. Beginning in January 2000, Creal began to spend nights at his wife's apartment with her children in Troy, Kansas. He progressively moved his clothes, furniture, photo albums and other memorabilia into the apartment, slept each night in the apartment, and split the cost of the utilities and paying the grocery bills. By July 2000, the two were married. Two weeks before his death, Creal and his second wife purchased a home in Kansas. However, Creal retained certain connections with the State of Missouri: he registered his motor vehicles in Missouri, maintained a Missouri driver's license and continued to receive mail and his paycheck stubs at his mother's Missouri address. Following his death, an estate was opened in a Missouri court, alleging that he resided at his mother's Missouri address.

I

Was Creal a citizen of Kansas at the time of his death, notwithstanding the fact that he retained certain connections with the State of Missouri?

R

A party's domicile is that place in which the party has established a physical presence with the intent to remain there.

A

Federal diversity jurisdiction exists only when the case involves parties with complete diversity of citizenship. Citizenship is established by the state in which a party is ***domiciled***. A party's domicile is that place in which the party has "established a physical presence" with the "intent to remain there." In the instant case, defendants challenge plaintiff's factual assertion that Creal was a citizen of Missouri, not Kansas, at the time of his death. We disagree. Although Creal had some connection to the state of Missouri, those connections are too insignificant to overcome the evidence that his actions demonstrated an intent to remain with his wife and her children in Kansas. Creal had been living with his wife and two children in Kansas, moved his belongings there and contributed to the rent and paid the grocery bills. Shortly before his death, he purchased a new home there. Therefore, because Creal had established a physical presence in Kansas with the intention to remain there, he was a Kansas citizen. Thus, because the defendants are also citizens of the same state [Kansas], federal diversity requirement have not been met [there is not complete diversity of citizenship] and the court lacks subject matter jurisdiction.

C

Motion granted.

Bridges v. Diesel Service Inc.

U.S. Dist. LEXIS 9429 (E.D. Pa. 1994)

FACTS

Plaintiff James Bridges sued Diesel Services, Inc. (defendant), his former employer, under the Americans with Disabilities Act ("ADA") claiming that defendant had terminated his employment in violation of the Act. The ADA requires that all administrative actions be exhausted before a discrimination suit can be brought; however, defendant's attorney failed to do so before filing her complaint. Specifically, she failed to file a charge with the Equal Employment Opportunity Commission ("EEOC") as required by the ADA. The court thus dismissed the complaint and defendant moved for sanctions under Rule 11(c), claiming that Bridges had violated Rule 11(b)(2). That provision provides that before presenting a complaint to the court, the attorney is certifying that to the best of his knowledge, the pleading is supported by a reasonable factual investigation and a normally competent level of legal research and that the claims in the complaint are warranted by existing law. Under Rule 11(c), a court may award sanctions for a Rule 11 violation – payment of the moving party's legal expenses.

I

Must a court impose sanctions under Rule 11(c) for a Rule 11(b) violation?

R

Rule 11 sanctions are designed to deter improper conduct and will only be applied in exceptional circumstances where the claim is patently frivolous and substantive in nature and generally do not include procedural errors.

A

A court need not impose Rule 11 sanctions for each and every violation of Rule 11(b). Rule 11 sanctions are designed to deter improper conduct and will only be applied in exceptional circumstances where the claim is patently frivolous and substantive in nature and generally do not include procedural errors. An attorney's signature is a certification that the pleading is supported by a reasonable amount of factual investigation and a competent level of legal research. A violation of Rule 11(b) occurs if, in light of the above, the signing the complaint is objectively unreasonable under the circumstances. Here, plaintiff's attorney did not demonstrate a competent level of research; if she had, she would have discovered the EEOC filing requirement after even a brief inspection of the ADA requirements. However, while Rule 11 sanctions have been imposed at times for a failure to exhaust administrative remedies, such admonishment is not appropriate here. Rule 11 is designed to deter improper conduct and in this case there is no evidence that sanctions are necessary to deter future improper conduct by plaintiff's attorney. Plaintiff's attorney immediately acknowledged her error and promptly filed the charge with the EEOC. Plaintiff's complaint was dismissed and we are convinced that she has learned her lesson and will demonstrate a greater level of due diligence in the future.

C

Motion for sanctions denied.

Bell v. Novick Transfer Co.

17 F.R.D. 279 (D. Md. 1955)

FACTS

Plaintiff Ronald Bell, a minor, was injured after the car he was riding in was broad-sided by a tractor-trailer. The truck was owned by Defendants Novick Transfer Company and Katie Marie Parsons and was operated by Morris Jarrett Coburn, III, also a defendant in the instant action. Plaintiff filed a negligence claim in state court [Maryland], but the case was removed to federal court on defendants' motion. Defendants then moved to dismiss the case arguing that plaintiff's complaint failed to state a claim under which relief could be granted; that is, he did not allege any specific act of negligence which resulted in an injury. The complaint alleged that on August 14, 1954, the infant plaintiff was riding in a car on Race Road in Baltimore County, Maryland when it was struck on the passenger side by a tractor-trailer truck owned by defendants Novick and Parsons and operated by defendant Coburn at the intersection of Race Road and Pulaski Highway. The declaration also alleges Bell's injuries and damages and asserted that they were caused as a direct result of defendants' negligence.

I Is a federal court required to apply Rule 12(e), a state rule requiring "a more definite statement," if the case originated in state court but was subsequently removed to federal court?

R A federal court is not required to apply a state "well-pleaded complaint" rule even when the case originated in state court under state substantive law.

A Rule 8 of the Federal Rules of Civil Procedure requires only that a complaint be "a short and plain statement of the claim showing that the pleader is entitled to relief." As such, a defendant is not entitled to a "more definite statement" under Rule 12(e) because the information plaintiff would have to provide can be obtained during the discovery phase of the litigation. Thus, plaintiff's complaint satisfies this requirement by alleging negligence on defendants' part and asserting that negligence attributable to them caused the plaintiff's injuries.

C Motion to dismiss denied.

Larson v. American Family Insurance Co.

2007 U.S. Dist. LEXIS 41864 (D. Colo. 2007)

FACTS

Plaintiffs "the Larsons" retained an attorney, defendant Brad Ross-Shannon, to sue American Family Mutual Insurance Company, which held their homeowners' policy, after the company failed to pay a house fire claim. Ross-Shannon did not pursue their claim because he was trying to be hired by American Family in other matters. The Larsons fired Ross-Shannon and hired another attorney, who initially filed a complaint in April 2006 against only American Family, in state court. American Family removed the case to federal court on the basis of diversity jurisdiction. After the insurance company provided discovery in January 2007, the Larsons learned that Ross-Shannon was in talks with the company (D) while he was representing the Larsons. The Larsons attorney then sought to amend their complaint to add Ross-Shannon (D) as an additional defendant, based on breach of fiduciary duty, legal malpractice, and conspiracy, claims that would destroy diversity and force a remand to state court. Ross-Shannon and American Family (D) objected.

I

(1) Is an amendment to a complaint seeking to join a party to a lawsuit that is filed one month after complainant confirms the party's involvement in the lawsuit timely filed under the FRCP; (2) May all persons be joined in one action as defendants if claims against them arise out of the same transaction or occurrence as the other claims?

R

(1) An amendment to a complaint seeking to join a party to a lawsuit that is filed one month after complainant confirms the party's involvement in the lawsuit is timely filed under the FRCP. (2) All persons may be joined in one action as defendants if claims against them arise out of the same transaction or occurrence as the other claims.

A

(1) Yes. An amendment to a complaint seeking to join a party to a lawsuit that is filed one month after complainant confirms the party's involvement in the lawsuit is timely filed under the Federal Rules of Civil Procedure. The Larsons (P) may have suspected that Ross-Shannon (D) was negotiating with American Family (D) before February 2006, but could not confirm that it was so until American Family (D) provided discovery in January 2007. (2) Yes. All persons may be joined in one action as defendants if claims against them arise out of the same transaction or occurrence as the other claims. The breach of their respective duties arise out of the same occurrence or transaction, or series of occurrences or transactions, and it would be inefficient to have one set of claims tried against American Family (D) in federal court and another set tried against the lawyer (D) in state court. Joinder is therefore proper.

C

Remanded to state court.

Butler v. Rigby

1998 U.S. Dist. LEXIS 4618 (E.D. La. 1998)

FACTS

Plaintiff Butler and the other plaintiffs in the case received medical treatment from the American Medical Group ("AMG") and from Midtown Health Center ("MHC") for injuries relating to an automobile accident. Defendant Rigsby served AMG and MHC with notices of depositions requesting documents and other information including (1) a listing of the total number of patients treated by AMG and MHC since 1992 that are now involved in the instant ; (2) a listing of the total number of patients treated by AMG and MHC since 1992 which have been referred to you by attorneys; (3) a list of patients referred to AMG and MHC by specific personal-injury lawyers and (4) any letters of guarantee or contacts with attorneys of law firms relating to individuals seen. ANG and MHC moved for a protective order prohibiting Rigsby's discovery on the grounds that the list of patients referred by certain personal-injury lawyers was not relevant to the lawsuit under Rule 26(b)(1), that the listing of the number of current AMG and MHC patients was protected by the doctor-patient privilege, and that the request for information was unduly burdensome under Rule 26(b)(2) and (c). Rule 26(c) allows individuals from whom discovery is sought to move for a protective order even if they are not parties to the suit. Rule 26(b)(1) allows parties to obtain discovery "regarding any matter, not privileged, which is relevant to the subject matter involved in the pending action." Rule 26 (b)(2) allows courts to restrict discovery if "the burden or expense of the proposed discovery outweighs its likely benefit." The magistrate judge denied AMG's and MHC's motion.

I

Can the doctor-patient privilege or the attorney-client privilege protect certain information from discovery when such information is both relevant to the case under Rule 26(b)(1) and not unduly burdensome under Rule 26(b)(2)?

R

A legal privilege can be used to protect information from discovery under Rule 26.

A

A ***legal*** privilege can protect certain information from discovery, even when the information is relevant to the subject of the lawsuit under Rule 26(b)(1) and the request was not unduly burdensome under Rule 26(b)(2). However, discovery can be limited when the request for information "is unreasonably cumulative or duplicative" or where the burden or expense proposed by the discovery outweighs its likely benefit. Here, AMG and MHC argued that the listing of all patients referred by certain personal-injury lawyers was both irrelevant and burdensome. On the other hand, Rigsby (defendant) argued that the information was necessary to establish that AMG and MHC had received substantial income from attorneys who had represented Butler, and that such evidence was relevant to show bias on their part. Evidence of a "special relationship" between an attorney and his expert witness is relevant to establishing bias and discovery that is designed to expose

---

such bias should be allowed when the request for information is not too burdensome. In this case, the burden imposed on AMG and MHC does not outweigh the likely benefit to defendant. However, because AMG and MHC will expend considerable expense to such lists, the Court orders that Rigsby will have to pay half of AMG and MHC's costs to do so. We now turn to the request for the list of patients treated by AMG and MHC since 1992; a list that would include a list of both current and past patients. Under Louisiana case law, the identities of a health care provider's past and current patients are protected by the doctor-patient privilege and are therefore not discoverable under Rule 26(b)(1). But even if this were not the case, we do not see how the identity of these patients could be relevant to the lawsuit at hand.

C Affirmed in part and reversed in part.

Houchens v. American Home Assurance Co.

927 F.2d 163 (4th Cir. 1991)

FACTS

In 1980, Coulter Houchens disappeared in August 1980 while vacationing in Bangkok, Thailand. According to Thai immigration records, Mr. Houchens arrived in Bangkok on August 15, 1980. His entry permit was valid only until August 29. No one has heard from Mr. Houchens since his that time. The State Department, FBI, ICAO, Red Cross, and Mrs. Houchens (plaintiff) searched for him. All efforts to locate him were fruitless. In 1988 a Virginia court issued an order declaring that Mr. Houchens was legally dead under Virginia law and Mrs. Houchens (plaintiff) then filed a claim with American Home Assurance Company (defendant), the provider of Mr. Houchens' two accidental death policies. American refused to pay under these policies arguing that there was no evidence that Mr. Houchens had died by accident. Mrs. Houchens sued for breach of contract, and American moved for summary judgment. The district court granted the motion on the grounds that Mrs. Houchens did not proffer sufficient evidence that would allow a jury reasonably to find that Mr. Houchens was dead or that if he was such a fatality resulted from an accident.

I

Where evidence is proffered which presumes but does not prove the issue at hand [here that the deceased occurred by accident], can a motion for summary judgment be defeated?

R

A legal presumption cannot be used to defeat a motion for summary judgment and an "appellate court must grant summary judgment when it appears from the record that there is an unresolved issue of material fact . . . viewed in the light most favorable to the party opposing the motion."

A

Under §64.1-105 of the Virginia Code, a person who has been missing for seven years is presumed to be dead. However, in order to recover from the deceased's insurance carrier, defendant American Home Assurance Company, Mrs. Houchens must prove that Mr. Houchens' death was caused by accident. The district court granted summary judgment to the defendant-insurance co. applying the rule developed by the U.S. Supreme Court in *Celotex Corp. v. Catrett*. Under that rule, the court should grant a motion for summary judgment against a party "who fails to make a showing sufficient to establish the existence of an element essential to that party's case." "[A]n appellate court must therefore reverse the grant of summary judgment if it appears from the record that there is an unresolved issue of material fact . . . viewed in the light most favorable to the party opposing the motion," *Helm v. Western Maryland Ry. Co.* Here, Mrs. Houchens argues that the presumption that Mr. Houchens is dead was enough to meet her burden of proving that Mr. Houchens died accidentally and bases her argument on three cases decided outside the 4th Circuit; none of which can be readily distinguishable from the case at bar: unlike the three cases cited by the plaintiff, here there is only evidence of a disappearance, not of an accident. A jury could conclude that Mr. Houchens disappeared, and presume that he died under Virginia law, but there is no evidence that would allow a jury to conclude that Mr. Houchens died as a result of an accident. Viewed in the light most favorable to the plaintiff, we can only conclude that the deceased disappeared, and then presume that he died under Virginia law. We cannot, however, conclude that he died accidentally. To conclude otherwise would be to pile "inference upon inference."

C

Affirmed.

Norton v. Snapper Power Equipment

806 F.2d 1545 (11th Cir. 1987)

FACTS

Plaintiff James L. Norton was in the commercial lawn mowing business. He bought a riding mower manufactured by Snapper Power Equipment (defendant) in 1981. Three years later, while he was using the riding mower to clear leaves from a yard which was adjacent to a creek. As he drove the mower up an incline [away from a creek], the mower began to reverse. It did not respond when Norton tried to brake, and he and it eventually crashed into the creek. Norton caught his hand in the mower's blades and lost four of his fingers. After plaintiff presented his case, Snapper moved for a ***directed verdict*** on all counts. The court dismissed all of Norton's claims but the strict liability claim. Norton's strict liability claim was that defendant failed to install a safety device called a "dead man" device, which would have stopped the engine from running; the absence of which rendered it defective. This so-called defect, claimed the plaintiff, was the cause of his injury. The jury found for Norton on the strict liability claim, but the court decided to enter a ***judgment notwithstanding the verdict*** [j.n.o.v.], holding that the jury could not reasonably have found that a Snapper mower had a defect that was the cause of Norton's injury because Norton (plaintiff) did not present sufficient evidence that there was a defect in the mower at the time he bought it.

I

Can a court grant a j.n.o.v after it has already denied to grant a motion for a directed verdict based on the same facts?

R

A j.n.o.v cannot be granted after a motion for a directed verdict has been denied based on the same facts.

A

The test for a judgment notwithstanding the verdict is the same as the test for a directed verdict. The court must consider the evidence presented in the light most favorable to the nonmoving party and should grant the judgment only when the evidence points so strongly in favor of the moving party that a reasonable jury could not arrive at a contrary verdict. Here, plaintiff Norton argues that the Snapper mower was unreasonably dangerous because it did not have a "dead man" device. Defendant Snapper argued that because plaintiff Norton did not know exactly how his hand got caught in the mower's blades, the jury could not have determined that the "dead man" safety switch would have prevented Norton's injury. Snapper correctly points out that plaintiff "is not entitled to a verdict based on speculation and conjecture." The jury is, however, permitted to decide on the facts by drawing inference upon inference. In *Fenner v. General Motors Corp.,* the district court granted a judgment notwithstanding the verdict in a case where the plaintiff argued that his injuries were caused when a defective steering mechanism caused his car to swerve off the highway after a stone became lodged in it. In that case, because plaintiff's vehicle was not examined by experts and because the experts that did testify could only state that it was “theoretically possible” that a stone became lodged in the plaintiff's steering mechanism, the court rightfully entered a judgment notwithstanding the verdict. In this case, however, the causation evidence is much stronger. Norton testified that his mower reversed into the creek and expert testimony verified that a "dead man" safety device would have stopped the blades in less than a second. By contrast, the blades in Snapper mower Norton was using took two or three seconds to stop. Thus, a reasonable jury ***could*** have concluded that a "dead man" device ***could*** have prevented Norton's injury.

C

See above.

Rush v. City of Maple Heights

Supreme Court of Ohio, 147 N.E.2d 599 (1958)

FACTS

The plaintiff sued the defendant in a Cleveland municipal court when she was injured in a motorcycle accident. The plaintiff (Rush) claimed the defendant (City of Maple Heights) was negligent in maintaining the street and that this negligence was the proximate cause of her damages. The trial court awarded her damages of $100. The plaintiff appealed, but the judgment was affirmed by the Ohio Court of Appeals and the Ohio Supreme Court. Plaintiff Rush also brought this action in the Court of Common Pleas of Cuyahoga for the personal injuries she suffered in the same accident. Rush moved to set trial on the issues of damages alone. The court granted this motion on the grounds that the issue of negligence was *res judicata* because of the municipal court action. The Cuyahoga court entered judgment on a verdict for $12,000 for the plaintiff. The Court of Appeals affirmed.

I

Can more than one cause of action for damages (personal injuries and property damage) resulting from one accident be maintained by a plaintiff?

R

A plaintiff may maintain only one action to enforce his rights existing at the time such action is commenced.

A

A plaintiff may maintain only one action to enforce his rights existing at the time such action is commenced. The *Vasu* Rule is inapplicable to the case at hand and should not be followed. The rule presented in *Vasu v. Kohlers* states that the recovery or denial of recovery of compensation for damages to property is not a bar to a subsequent action for personal injury from same wrongful act unless adverse judgment in first action would affect issue in second action. The *Vasu* Rule should not be followed because it is in conflict with the great weight of legal authority in this country. Normally, the injuries to persons and property are the derivative results of a single, wrongful act, but a single tort can be the basis of but one action. To permit otherwise would unleash a multiple of suits causing significant delays for all of the parties, thereby purging judicial efficiency.

C

Judgment reversed with the final judgment for the defendant (City of Maple Heights).

Apex Hosiery Co. v. Leader

102 F.2d 702 (3rd Cir. 1939)

FACTS

Defendant Leader, a labor union, appeals from an order of the court below made under Rule 34 for the discovery and production of documents for inspection, copying, and photographing by Apex Hosiery Co., the plaintiff in this antitrust action. Defendant objected, and the lower court issued an order requiring that it produce the documents.

I

Can a party appeal a federal court order to produce documents under Rule 34?

R

An order to produce information under Rule 34 cannot be appealed.

A

An order to produce documents for the inspection, copying, and photographing of the opposing party is an interlocutory order and, therefore, not appealable, as expressly decided by the Supreme Court in *Cogen v. United States*. The rational behind this rule is that only orders that have the effect of ending the case in favor of one party or the other can be appealed, with one exception: orders that punish parties criminally for contempt; these orders do not effectively end the trial and can be appealed. In this case, the order to produce documents will not cause the final disposition of the case in favor of Apex Hosiery (plaintiff) or Leader (defendant), and is therefore not appealable under *Cogen*.

C

See Rule above.

Pennoyer v. Neff

U.S Supreme Court, 95 U.S. 714 (1877)

FACTS

Neff (plaintiff) sought to recover possession of land which was seized and sold to pay off a default judgment against him. Plaintiff Neff claimed that the default judgment was invalid because the issuing court did not have personal jurisdiction over him. Long before the suit, Neff apparently never paid for legal services rendered by John Mitchell and Mitchell sued Neff in Oregon state court to recover his unpaid fees. Mitchell did not personally serve Neff but published notice of the suit in a local newspaper. Mitchell obtained a default judgment against Neff and obtained his land at an auction where Mitchell was the "lucky bidder." Neff, not being an Oregon resident at the time, did not know of the default judgment and seizure of his land. A few days later, Mitchell assigned the newly acquired land to Pennoyer (defendant). Pennoyer spent 9 years improving the property only to have Neff show up claiming the land was his. Neff sued Pennoyer in federal court and got his land back. Pennoyer appealed the decision to the Supreme Court but was unsuccessful and Neff remained in possession of the land.

I

Can a state court exercise personal jurisdiction over a non state resident who has not been properly served with process and whose property within the state was not attached in any court proceeding?

R

States may enter a binding judgment against non-residents only if they are personally served within the state's border or if they have property within the state. Every state possesses exclusive sovereignty over persons and property with its boarders.

A

Every state possesses exclusive sovereignty over persons and property with its boarders. States may enter a binding judgment against non residents only if they are personally served within the state's boarder or if they have property within the state. A state may obtain *in personam* jurisdiction over a non-resident only if he is properly served within the state. *In personam* jurisdiction allows a state to have power over the person. A state may obtain *in rem* jurisdiction over a non resident only if he has property within the state. *In Rem* jurisdiction allows a state to have power over an individual's property.

C

Judgment affirmed.

International Shoe Co. v. Washington

U.S. Supreme Court, 326 U.S. 310 (1945)

FACTS

International Shoe Co. (defendant), a Delaware incorporated company, had its primary place of business in St. Louis, Missouri. It maintained a number of salesmen in Washington State but did not have any offices there. Plaintiff (State of Washington) pursuant to its state laws served notice on the salesmen in a suit involving the collection of unemployment taxes. International Shoe challenged the service claiming it was not present or doing business in Washington State and therefore was not subject to he state's jurisdiction. The Unemployment Office, the Commissioner, the Superior Court and the Supreme Court of Washington all found that the service was proper. Thereafter, International Shoe appealed to the U.S. Supreme Court.

I

If a corporation has "minimum contacts" with a state, but not incorporated there, is it still subject to that state's jurisdiction?

R

A corporation is subject to a state's jurisdiction if it has "minimum contacts" with the state; even if it is not incorporated in that particular state.

A

Generally, "systematic and continuous activities" constitute minimum contacts within the state. However, courts have sometimes held that even one phone call may constitute a "minimum contact" if the quality is high enough. The public policy behind this reasoning is as follows: If a corporation enjoys the benefits that a particular state has to offer (its court system, laws, customers, etc.) it should be subject to the state's jurisdiction.

C

Yes. A corporation is subject to a state's jurisdiction if it has "minimum contacts" with the state; even if it is not incorporated in that particular state.

McGee v. International Life Insurance Co.

U.S. Supreme Court, 355 U.S. 220 (1957)

FACTS

Plaintiff McGee, the beneficiary of a life insurance policy, brought suit in California against Defendant International Life, a Texas company, when the latter refused to pay according to the terms of an insurance policy. The Defendant refused the payout claiming policy holder Lowell Franklin committed suicide and therefore beneficiary McGee was not entitled to the proceeds. The plaintiff brought suit in California, under a state law that authorized service of process on out-of-state companies which had in-state contracts with in-state residents. After winning a judgment in California court, plaintiff tried to enforce the judgment in a Texas court. The Texas court, however, refused to give full faith and credit to the judgment (e.g. refused to enforce the judgment in Texas) because the Texas court claimed that California's exercise of jurisdiction was improper. Thereafter, the Texas decision was appealed to the U.S. Supreme Court by Plaintiff McGee.

I Where a contact with a state is limited to a single act, can a state exercise jurisdiction over a defendant?

R A state may exercise jurisdiction over a defendant when the contact with that state is limited to a single act or contract, provided that the act was: (1) deliberately directed toward the state; and (2) the act is what gave rise to the claim for which jurisdiction is being sought.

A As a public policy matter, it is more likely that small policy holders would be denied justice if they were forced to file suit in a foreign jurisdiction. This is why California enacted its long arm statute; to protect the rights of its citizens from out-of-state insurance companies. The inconvenience arising out of defending a suit in California (as opposed to Texas) would not rise to the level of a denial of Due Process given that International Life had actual notice of the suit and ample time to prepare a defense in a California Court.

C Yes. A state may exercise jurisdiction over a defendant when the contact with that state is limited to a single act or contract, provided that the act was (1) deliberately directed toward the state; and (2) the act is what gave rise to the claim for which jurisdiction is being sought. Judgment reversed.

Hanson v. Denckla

U.S. Supreme Court, 357 U.S. 235 (1958)

FACTS

Dora Donner set up a trust with a Delaware bank as trustee (assumed to be the defendant). She was a resident of Pennsylvania, but eventually moved to Florida where she established a will naming her two daughters as primary *heirs*. That same day, she named two of her grandchildren *beneficiaries* of the trust. When she died a few years later, the two daughters brought suit against the Trustee, the Delaware Bank, claiming the appointment of the beneficiaries was invalid and that the trust money should go to the estate (and eventually to each daughter via the will). While the Florida suit was pending, the two daughters filed a suit in Delaware. When the Florida court found for the two sisters (that the trust was invalid), the two daughters tried to introduce that judgment into the Delaware suit. The Delaware court held that the trust was valid and that the Florida court had no jurisdiction over the trust company. The U.S. Supreme Court consolidated the actions for review.

I Can a state exercise jurisdiction over a non-resident defendant when the contacts with the state do not give rise to the claim for which jurisdiction is sought?

R A state may not exercise jurisdiction over a non-resident defendant if the contacts with the state are insignificant and the claim does not arise from those contacts.

A Without some action "by which the defendant purposefully avails itself of the privilege of conducting activities within the forum state, thus invoking the benefits and protections of its laws," it cannot be said that the defendant has the requisite minimum contacts with that state. In the instant case, the Delaware trustee conducts no business in Florida, has no office there and conducts no business there. Therefore, Florida cannot exercise jurisdiction over the Delaware trustee. **DISSENT:** Florida had a strong interest in the litigation; Donner lived in Florida, her heirs lived in Florida and the Trustee was carrying on business with a Florida resident. The Trust company had the required minimum contacts with the State of Florida to justify Florida's jurisdiction over it.

C No. Mrs. Donner's contacts with Florida did not establish the prerequisite contacts necessary between the Delaware trustee and the state of Florida. Therefore, Florida cannot exercise jurisdiction over the Defendant Trustee. Judgment reversed.

Shaffer v. Heitner

U.S. Supreme Court, 433 U.S. 186 (1977)

FACTS

The plaintiff owned one share of stock in Greyhound Corp., a Delaware incorporated business. Heitner (plaintiff) was a non-resident of the State of Delaware. Heitner filed a shareholder's derivative suit in Delaware court alleging that the officers of the corporation had breached their fiduciary duty to the shareholders. Plaintiff filed for a sequestration of approximately 82,000 shares held collectively by 21 officers and directors of the company. The 21 defendants entered a special appearance in Delaware contending that the sequestration violated due process and that the property could not be attached in Delaware. That is, the 21 defendants asserted that they did not have the requisite minimum contacts with Delaware to justify Delaware's jurisdiction over them. The Delaware Court of Chancery rejected their arguments and the Delaware Supreme Court affirmed. The Supreme Court of the United States granted Certiorari.

I

Must the requisite "minimum contacts" exist for a court to exercise *in rem* jurisdiction?

R

"Minimum contacts" must exist for a court to exercise its *in rem* jurisdiction over a defendant in its jurisdiction.

A

Since the assertion of jurisdiction over the property is really just an assertion of jurisdiction over the owner of the property, the court concluded that all assertions of state court jurisdiction must be analyzed according to the standard enumerated in *International Shoe* and those cases that follow. In the instant case, Delaware has a strong interest in the litigation (the Corporation is incorporated in Delaware) but the requisite minimum contacts do not exist. The officers and directors have not purposefully availed themselves of the protections of the state, nor have they ever set foot within the state. **DISSENT:** Agreed with the minimum contact analysis but disagreed with the ultimate holding of the case. The minimum contacts analysis should be applied; however, the majority treated Delaware's statute as a long arm statute requiring a" minimum contacts" analysis but the Delaware statute expressly denied such an approach.

C

Yes. "Minimum contacts" must exist for a court to exercise its *in rem* jurisdiction over a defendant in its jurisdiction.

World Wide Volkswagen Corp. v. Woodson

U.S. Supreme Court, 444 U.S. 286 (1980)

FACTS

In the mid-seventies, the Robinsons, a New York family, purchased an Audi from co-Defendant Seaway Volkswagen (a car dealership) in New York. As the Robinsons were traveling to their new home in Arizona, they were rear-ended while passing through the state of Oklahoma. The two children and their mother, Kay, were severely injured when the Audi's gas tank ruptured and the car caught fire. The Robinsons filed suit in Oklahoma state court against the car's importer, Volkswagen of America; its regional distributor, World Wide Volkswagen and Seaway, the N.Y. dealership. Seaway challenged the Oklahoma court's jurisdiction claiming an absence of "minimum contacts" since it did business only in New York. Co-defendant World Wide Volkswagen also challenged the Oklahoma Court's jurisdiction since it claimed only to do business in the tri-state New York area. Nonetheless, the Okalahoma court held for the Robinsons and the case was appealed to the Supreme Court of the United States.

I

Can a state exercise jurisdiction over a defendant if the defendant has not deliberately sought contacts with the state but where the state would be the most convenient forum to try the case (all witness are there, plaintiffs were injured and treated there, the claim arose there and the defendant can conveniently defend itself there)?

R

A defendant must have some contact with the form state in order to be subject to the state's jurisdiction. Issues of fairness, convenience and the interests of the state in overseeing the litigation are irrelevant.

A

Minimum contacts must be based on some act committed by the defendant. In the instant case, it is reasonable to believe that neither Defendant Seaway nor Defendant World Wide Volkswagen expected to be brought before an Oklahoma court. Neither defendant had ever conducted business in Oklahoma nor intended their products to reach the Oklahoma consumer. Therefore, the "minimum contacts" test is not satisfied and the judgment is reversed. **DISSENT:** While the contacts were not extensive between Defendants Seaway and World Wide Volkswagen and Oklahoma, other factors such as fairness and convenience must be considered as it would have been easy for both defendants to defend in Oklahoma without too much inconvenience.

C

No. A state cannot exercise jurisdiction over a defendant who has not deliberately sought some contact with the forum state. Judgment Reversed.

Asahi Metal Industry Co. v. Superior Court

U.S. Supreme Court, 480 U.S. 102 (1987)

FACTS

In 1978, Gary and Ruth Zurcher were involved in a motorcycle accident which seriously injured Gary and killed his wife, Ruth. Gary Zurcher filed suit in California against Defendant Cheng Shin Rubber Industrial Co., the tire tube manufacturer of the motorcycle, who in turn filed a cross claim for indemnification against the then defendant, Asahi Metal Industry Co., the Japanese manufacturer of the tire tube's valve assembly. Zurcher eventually settled with Cheng Shin Rubber leaving Chen Shin's cross claim against Asahi Metal. Asahi defended on the basis that it never did business in California, such that California could not exert jurisdiction over it (Asahi clamed no minimum contacts existed between it and California). The trial court ruled against Asahi holding that it was an international company and therefore subject to California's jurisdiction. The Court of Appeals disagreed and reversed. The Supreme Court of California sided with the trial court against Asahi (plaintiff on appeal) and Asahi appealed to the Supreme Court of the United States.

I

In order to establish "minimum contacts" with a forum state, is it sufficient to put a product into the stream of commerce with the expectation that it reach the forum state?

R

The defendant must "purposely avail himself of the forum state" by more than putting a product into the stream of commerce, in order to trigger the "minimum contacts" requirement.

A

Something more than placing a product into the stream of commerce is necessary to establish "minimum contacts" between the defendant and the forum state. There mere fact that a product might find its way into the state's market alone is not enough. The defendant must have performed some deliberate act intending to take advantage of the state laws and/or the local market. He must have intentionally placed his products into the "stream of commerce" with the knowledge and intent that they reach the California marketplace.

C

No. In order to establish "minimum contacts" with a forum state, the defendant must have intentionally placed his product(s) into the "stream of commerce" with the expectation that those products reach the forum state. Reversed and remanded.

Burger King Corp. v. Rudzewicz

U.S. Supreme Court, 471 U.S. 462 (1985)

FACTS

The defendant and his partner entered into a franchise agreement with the Burger King Corporation (plaintiff), a Florida Corporation. Both partners were residents of Michigan. The contract stipulated that the agreement would be governed by Florida law and for payment of all franchise fees to be made to Burger King's Miami Headquarters. After falling behind on some payments, Burger King filed suit in Florida Federal court. Defendant John Rudzewicz and his partner Brian MacShara claimed they did not have the requisite minimum contacts with Florida to be subject to Florida's jurisdiction. The District Court found Florida could exercise jurisdiction and the Court of Appeals reversed holding that although defendants did have the necessary contacts with Florida, such jurisdiction would be inherently unfair and would set a dangerous precedent. The plaintiff appealed to the Supreme Court of the United States.

I

In asserting jurisdiction, must a state show BOTH minimum contacts with the forum state AND that it would be fair and equitable to require defendants to defend there?

R

Once minimum contacts have been established, the burden shifts to the defendant to prove the defense of the suit in the forum state is "fundamentally unfair."

A

While the state does not have to show both minimum contacts and that it would be fair and equitable for the defendant to defend a suit there, there is a presumption that the defense of the suit would be fair and equitable. This presumption can be overcome by a showing of unfairness by the defendant. Defendant Rudzewicz, while never having set foot in Florida, had actual notice that Burger King might sue him there as those were the terms of the franchise contract which he signed. Florida is the most convenient forum to try the case because Berger King is a Florida Corporation, governed by Florida law. Moreover, Defendant Rudzewicz has not proven that he would be unfairly prejudiced or harmed by defending a suit in Florida. Thus, defendant's due process rights were not oppressed.

C

No. A state need not show both "minimum contacts" with the forum state AND that it would be fair and equitable to require a defendant to defend there in asserting jurisdiction over one of the parties. Reversed and remanded.

Pavlovich v. Superior Court

29 Cal. 4th 262, 58 P.3d 2 (2002)

FACTS

Petitioner Pavlovich (defendant), a current Texas resident and the president of Media Driver, LLC, studied at Purdue University in Indiana and was employed in Indiana as a systems and network administrator prior to moving to Texas. He never resided or worked in California, owned property in California, maintained a place of business in California, or otherwise had any contacts with the state of California. While in Indiana, Pavlovich founded and was the project leader of the LiVid video project, which operated a Web site containing text and links to other Web sites. The Web site contained a single page, and only provided information. It neither solicited nor transacted any business. It was simply designed to provide information to those interested in improving "video and DVD support for Linux." To that end, the website sought to defeat the CSS encryption technology which prevented the copying and pirating of DVDs. To reach this goal, the website posted the source code of a program that could be used to bypass the encrypted data on the copyrighted DVDs and allow for their free copying. DVD Copy Control Association, Inc. (plaintiff), a Delaware corporation with its principal place of business in California, owned the licensing rights to the CSS encryption technology. Although Pavlovich was aware that posting the code was probably illegal and "heard" that a there was a place to apply got a license, he was unaware that plaintiff owned the licensing rights to the CSS technology. Plaintiff sued Pavlovich in California state court for misappropriating trade secrets through his Web site. The complaint sought injunctive relief only, and was not a claim for monetary damages. Pavlovich filed a motion to quash service of process, contending that the California court lacked personal jurisdiction. That motion was denied, and the California Supreme Court heard the appeal.

I Does a California court have personal jurisdiction over a nonresident defendant whose only connection to the state is that information posted to a Web site which results in injury to a California resident?

R A court may exercise personal jurisdiction over a nonresident defendant ***only*** if (1) the defendant has purposefully availed himself of the benefits of the forum state, (2) the action relates to the defendant's contacts with the forum state, and (3) jurisdiction would not offend "notions of fair play and substantial justice."

A A court may exercise personal jurisdiction over a nonresident defendant ***only*** if (1) the defendant has purposefully availed himself of the benefits of the forum state, (2) the action relates to the defendant's contacts with the forum state, and (3) jurisdiction would not offend "notions of fair play and substantial justice." Generally, a party purposefully avails itself of a forum state if the foreseeable effects of the out-of-state action would be to injure a person within the forum state. Here, defendant's only contact with California is through the publication of material on his website which can be accessed by any Internet user in any state, including California. Although some courts have found that reaching out to a foreign state through the Internet may be a proper basis for personal jurisdiction, such jurisdiction is generally based on (1) the repeated transmission of computer files over the internet with knowledge by the defendant that contact is being made with individuals in that foreign jurisdiction; (2) where the defendant does business over the internet; (3) the interactivity of the users and the commercial nature of the exchange of information is high. This was not the case here. Here, the website was merely informational. As such, it is insufficient to establish personal jurisdiction. Moreover, there is no evidence to even suggest that defendant specifically targeted California residents; or even that any California resident ever accessed the site. Although defendant was aware that his website ***may*** injure the owner of the licensing rights to the CSS encryption technology, he did not know the owner's identity, or the fact that such an entity maintained its principal place of business in California. Such general knowledge is considered insufficient to establish that defendant purposefully availed himself to that jurisdiction – to hold otherwise, it would have to have been shown that he ***should have known*** that his actions may well harm certain ***California*** interests. While knowledge that his actions ***may*** affect California interests may help support personal jurisdiction, it is insufficient, by itself, to establish such jurisdiction. To pursue an action against the defendant, plaintiff must sue in either Indiana or Texas.

C

Reversed and remanded.

Perkins v. Benguet Consolidated Mining Co.

U.S. Supreme Court, 342 U.S. 437 (1952)

FACTS

Plaintiff Perkins was a stockholder in Defendant Benguet Consolidated Mining Co.'s company, a Philippine corporation. Benguet had an office in Ohio, where the president maintained a place of work with two secretaries. Perkins sued Benguet in Ohio claiming the company had failed to issue her stock and pay her dividends. Defendant Benguet moved to quash the service of summons claiming a lack of jurisdiction. The Ohio courts granted the motion and Plaintiff Perkins appealed to the United States Supreme Court.

I

Where a defendant has minimum contacts with the forum state, but the cause of action does not arise out of those contacts, can a state still exercise jurisdiction over a defendant?

R

So long as there are "sufficient minimum" contacts with the forum state, a state may exercise jurisdiction over a defendant even when the cause of action does not arise out of those minimum contacts.

A

In the instant case, the defendant's contacts with the forum state were continuous, systemic and extensive. A state can exercise jurisdiction regardless of how or where the cause of action arose so long as the minimum contacts test is satisfied. Defendant Benguet's activities in Ohio were extensive and systematic because the President of the company maintained an office there. Moreover, the contacts were continuous as the office was permanent and the President and his two secretaries transacted company business at the site on a daily basis.

C

Yes. So long as there are sufficient minimum contacts with the forum state, a state may exercise jurisdiction over a defendant even when the cause of action does not arise out of those minimum contacts. Reversed and remanded.

Helicopters Nacionales de Columbia, S.A. v. Hall

U.S. Supreme Court, 466 U.S. 408437 (1983)

FACTS

The survivors and representatives of the decedents of a helicopter crash, including Plaintiff Hall, brought a wrongful death action in Texas against Defendant Helicopters Nacionales De Columbia, a Columbian corporation; Defendant Bell Helicopter, the helicopter's manufacturer and Defendants Consorcio, a Peruvian consortium and WSH, a joint venture headquartered in Houston, Texas. At the time of the accident, decedents were employed by defendants Consorcio and WSH who rented the helicopter from Defendant Helicol. Helicol opposed the jurisdiction of the court filed a special appearance. Thus, Helicol moved to dismiss the action arguing that its only contact with Texas consisted of sending its CEO to Houston to negotiate the rental contract and accept checks from Consorcio/WSH drawn on a Houston bank. The motion was denied and the jury returned a verdict in favor of Hall. The Texas appellate court reversed, citing *in personam* jurisdiction was lacking over Helicol. The Texas Supreme Court reversed again holding there was *in personam* jurisdiction over Helicol. The Supreme Court of the United States granted Certiorari.

I

Do negotiations and accepting checks in and/or from the forum state constitute "minimum contacts" sufficient to justify a state's exercise of *in personam* jurisdiction over a defendant?

R

So long as maintenance of the suite does not offend traditional notions of fair play and justice, personal jurisdiction may be satisfied by sufficient minimum contacts with the forum state.

A

Helicol's contacts with Texas did not constitute the type of systematic and continuous contacts with the state of Texas sufficient to constitute the exercise of *in personam* jurisdiction over the defendant. The one trip to Houston by the CEO for the purpose of negotiating a helicopter contract and accepting checks drawn on a Texas bank are not the type of "minimum contacts" which we consider to be systematic or continuous; rather they were a fairly isolated event. The mere acceptance of the checks cannot be considered sufficient for determining minimum contacts nor form a basis for personal jurisdiction over the defendant.

C

No. Negotiations and purchasing in the forum state do not constitute systematic and continuous contacts sufficient to justify the forum state's exercise of *in personam* jurisdiction over the defendant. Judgment reversed.

Burnham v. Superior Court

U.S. Supreme Court, 495 U.S. 604 (1990)

FACTS

The plaintiff sued her husband for divorce in a California state court. Plaintiff (Francie Burnham) was a resident of California, but her defendant-husband (Dennis Burnham) was not. The defendant was served with summons and complaint while he was visiting California for 3 days. The defendant asserted that his presence in California did not relate to the divorce action, and therefore moved to quash the service of process arguing that the California court lacked personal jurisdiction over him as his only contact with California were a few shorts trips for business and to visit his daughters. The California Court of Appeals denied the defendant's request for mandamus relief (a proceeding in superior court seeking an order to compel an inferior court to perform a duty; in this case, to quash the service of process) holding that physical presence alone coupled with proper personal service was enough to justify the state's jurisdiction over the defendant. The Supreme Court of the United States granted certiorari.

I

Does a court violate a defendant's due process rights if it obtains jurisdiction over a defendant via the defendant's physical appearance in the state?

R

Jurisdiction based on physical appearance in the state alone, regardless of the defendant's contacts with the forum state, is enough to justify a state's exercise of jurisdiction. In such a case, a person's due process rights are not violated.

A

Jurisdiction based on physical appearance alone satisfies due process because it is one of the continuing traditions of our U.S. legal system and because it conforms to "traditions notions of fair play and substantial justice." Only quasi *in rem* jurisdiction requires the minimum contacts analysis and does not compel the conclusion that a defendant's physical appearance in the state must be treated identically to those defendants who are absent.

C

No. Jurisdiction based on physical appearance in the state alone, regardless of the defendant's contacts with the forum state, is enough to justify a state's exercise of jurisdiction. Thus, a person's due process rights are not violated.

Carnival Cruise Lines Inc. v. Shute

U.S. Supreme Court, 499 U.S. 585 (1991)

FACTS

The plaintiffs purchased passenger tickets on the defendant's (Carnival Cruise Lines) cruise ship. Plaintiffs Eulala and Russel Schutte purchased these tickets in Washington from a ticket agent and payment was sent to the company's corporate headquarters in Florida. Each ticket contained a forum selection clause stating that all litigation was to be tried in a Florida court of law. While on the cruise ship, Mrs. Schutte was injured when she slipped on a deck mat. Plaintiffs filed suit in Washington District Court, alleging negligence and seeking damages. The District Court held that defendant's contacts in Washington were insufficient to establish jurisdiction over the defendant there. The Washington Court of Appeals reversed and the U.S. Supreme Court granted certiorari.

I

In establishing consent to jurisdiction over the defendant, is a reasonable forum selection clause enforceable?

R

Reasonable forum selection clauses are enforceable in establishing consent to jurisdiction.

A

It should be noted that the "minimum contacts" analysis is not applicable to the instant case because the forum selection clause was reasonable for several reasons: (1) the defendant has an interest in limiting the scope of potential litigants to a single forum, otherwise Carnival would be forced to litigate in possibly every state in the nation; (2) for efficiency reasons, the forum selection clause spares courts and litigants the time of preparing motions to determine the correct forum in which to litigate; and (3) passengers who buy tickets benefit from reduced fares as an indirect result of the savings defendant passes along to the purchaser as a result of defending actions in only one form. Therefore, the forum selection clause can be enforced, and the forum is proper in Florida.

C

Yes. Reasonable forum selection clauses are enforceable in establishing consent to jurisdiction.

Mullane v. Central Hanover Bank & Trust Co.

U.S. Supreme Court, 339 U.S. 306 (1950)

FACTS

Central Hanover Bank and Trust Company (plaintiff) established a trust fund which consisted of 113 smaller trust funds pooled together collectively for investment purposes. Plaintiff then petitioned New York's Surrogate Court for a judicial settlement naming itself as common trustee. Pursuant to New York law, all beneficiaries were notified by publication in a local newspaper for four consecutive weeks. Mullane (defendant) entered a special appearance in New York to object to the notice on the grounds that the notice should have been provided by mail and that the notice utilized was inadequate. The Surrogate Court over-ruled defendant's objections and both the Appellate Court of New York and the Court of Appeals (in New York, the Court of Appeals is the highest state court) affirmed. The Supreme Court of the United States granted certiorari.

I

Does notice by publication offend traditional due process requirements when the actual names and addresses of the parties are known in advance?

R

Notice by publication fails to comply with due process requirements when the names and the addresses of the parties are known in advance.

A

Due process requires that before a person's life, liberty or property is deprived, notice of adjudication is required. Notice provides an opportunity to be heard. In this case, the names and the addresses of the parties were known. It would be reasonable and not so burdensome to send actual notice to all of the beneficiaries and interested parties by mail since both their names and addresses were readily available. Furthermore, notice by publication is not a reliable method of notifying interested parties of their rights prior to a pending adjudication. Thus, notice by publication fails to comply with due process requirements in the present case.

C

No. Notice by publication fails to comply with due process requirements when the names and the addresses of the parties are known in advance.

Gibbons v. Brown

716 So. 2d 868 (Fl. Dist. Ct. App. 1998)

FACTS

In 1994 Martine Gibbons and Mr. and Mrs. Brown were driving together in Montreal, Canada. Gibbons (defendant) was a ***passenger*** in the car driven by Mr. Brown, and was sued by Mrs. Brown (plaintiff), also a passenger, for injuries sustained when their car collided head-on with another vehicle on a one-way street. Gibbons had given wrong directions to Mr. Brown, the driver of the car, which caused him to turn onto the one-way street, resulting in an accident. Gibbons was a Texas resident and Brown, a Florida resident. Mrs. Brown brought the action in Florida. She claims that Gibbons subjected herself to the personal jurisdiction of the Florida courts by bringing a prior lawsuit in Florida against ***Mr.*** Brown, the driver, two years earlier. However, she did not name ***Mrs.*** Brown as a defendant in that suit. Florida's long-arm statute provides that "a defendant who is engaged in substantial and not isolated activity within this state, whether such activity is wholly intrastate, interstate, or otherwise, is subject to the jurisdiction of the courts of this state, whether or not the claim arises from that activity." Defendant Gibbons challenges Florida's jurisdiction over her because her prior lawsuit did not include Mrs. Brown as a defendant, even though it involved the same accident and occurrence.

I

Can a court obtain jurisdiction over a non-resident defendant where the one and only contact with the state was the filing of a lawsuit two years earlier against a defendant not a party to the current suit?

R

Jurisdiction over a non-resident defendant is not proper where the only contact with the state was filing a lawsuit two years earlier against a defendant not a party to the current suit.

A

Under Florida's long-arm statute, a defendant must be "engaged in substantial and not isolated activity" within the state's jurisdiction. There is no showing by Brown (plaintiff) that Gibbons (defendant) "is engaged" in any activity in the state other than defending this lawsuit, which is insufficient without more. Moreover, the 2 year span between the two lawsuits and the fact that the prior suit did not name Brown (plaintiff) as a defendant, foreclose personal jurisdiction herein. We thus conclude that Brown (plaintiff) has not alleged a satisfactory ground for personal jurisdiction pursuant to Florida's long-arm statute.

C

The trial court is directed to dismiss plaintiff's complaint.

Dee-K Enterprises Inc. v. Heveafil Sdn. Bhd.

982 F. Supp. 1138 (E.D. Va. 1997)

FACTS

Dee-K Enterprises, Inc. (plaintiff) and other American purchasers of extruded rubber thread used in the making of bungee cords brought suit against various foreign governments and distributors of the thread alleging an international conspiracy to restrain trade in, and fix prices of, the thread in the United States. Heveafil Sdn. Bhd. (defendant) and other defendants moved to dismiss on the grounds of (1) lack of personal jurisdiction over a manufacturer from a foreign country, here an Indonesian manufacturer, where it consummates sales of the thread in the foreign country, and (2) improper venue in the Eastern District of Virginia.

I

Does the general ***federal*** venue statute subjecting alien corporations to suit in any judicial district override other ***federal*** statutes that may contain specific venue provisions, such as the one contained in §12 of the Clayton Act?

R

General federal venue statute subjecting alien corporations to suit in any judicial district overrides other federal statutes that may contain specific venue provisions.

A

Under 28 U.S.C. §1391 (d), a federal venue statute, aliens may be sued in any district. This statute overrides any special venue provision contained in other federal statutes such as the one contained in §12 of the Clayton Act. We are called upon today to address both personal jurisdiction and venue. With respect to personal jurisdiction, the prerequisites are well established. The standard to follow is that established in *International Shoe*. In that case, the U.S. Supreme Court the court held that personal jurisdiction over a non-resident defendant corporation exists where the defendant has certain minimum contacts with the state and maintenance of the suit does not offend traditional notions of fair play and substantial justice. To that end, we must initially determine whether under the federal statute or rule, due process is complied with pursuant to the "fair play and substantial justice." We find that due process was satisfied by defendant's appointment of exclusive U.S. sales agents and the customizing of its products for the U.S. markets. We now turn to the issue of venue. The antitrust statute, §12 of the Clayton Act, provides that venue is proper in any district where the defendant is "found" or where it "transacts business." Defendants [referring only to the foreign defendants in this action], however, conduct their business abroad. This fact is not fatal to establish proper venue, though, because the U.S. Supreme Court has held that the general federal venue statute, 28 U.S.C. § 1391 (d), which provides that aliens may be sued in any district, overrides any special venue provision contained in other federal statutes, here the antitrust laws. As to the American defendants, subsection (b) of 28 U.S.C. § 1391 provides that venue is proper, among other things, in a "judicial district in which any defendant may be found, if there is no district in which the action may otherwise be brought." Plaintiff has shown that some defendants have contact with Virginia so as to make venue proper in the ***Western*** District of Virginia; however, plaintiff must show that the contacts or businesses are located in the ***Eastern*** District of Virginia to make venue there proper as well.

C

See Rule above

Piper Aircraft v. Reyno

U.S. Supreme Court, 454 U.S. 235 (1981)

FACTS

Defendant Piper Aircraft manufactured commercial aircraft in Pennsylvania. One day, one of their aircraft crashed in the Scottish highlands and reports suggested that the airplane suffered from mechanical failure or pilot error or both. At the time of the crash, the airplane was registered in Great Britain and operated by a Scottish taxi service. Reyno (plaintiff), the estate administratrix to the attorney who filed on behalf of the Scottish families whose relatives had died, brought suit for wrongful death in California. Piper Aircraft (defendant) moved to transfer the case to Pennsylvania District Court and thereafter motioned to dismiss under the doctrine of *forum non conveniens* (doctrine in which the court has discretion over a case and may decline to exercise jurisdiction because not to do so would create a hardship on the defendant(s) or witnesses). The District Court granted the motion but the Circuit Court overruled it and remanded the case to trial in Pennsylvania. The court reasoned that the plaintiffs would be disadvantaged more by the law of Scotland then they would be by the law of Pennsylvania. The Supreme Court of the United States dismissed the case because the trial court did not have subject matter jurisdiction.

I

If the substantive law of an alternative forum is less favorable to the plaintiffs, should a motion to dismiss for *forum non conveniens* be denied?

R

When applying the doctrine of *forum non conveniens*, the fact that the substantive law of an alternate forum is less favorable to the plaintiffs should not be given conclusive or substantive weight.

A

If courts give weight to a change in substantive law, they will be forced to interpret the law of foreign jurisdictions in order to make a determination as to which forum is more favorable. The doctrine, however, was designed to avoid complex exercises in comparative law. Thus, a strong presumption exists to create a balancing test of public vs. private interests between plaintiffs and defendants to help to determine the appropriateness of a forum (see *Gulf Oil Corp. v Gilbert*). However, in the instant case it can be applied with less force since the plaintiffs are foreign. Great deference to a foreign plaintiff would encourage an onslaught of litigation in the U.S. court system. Moreover, the private policy interests indicate that that the District Court result should be upheld. This is because most of the witnesses and relevant evidence is collectively located in Great Britain. Lastly, public policy interests recommend a trial in Scotland because defendants Piper and Hartzell would have two different sets of law applied to them. Defendant Piper would be subject to Pennsylvania law whereas Hartzell would still be subject to Scottish law.

C

No. The fact that the substantive law of an alternate forum is less favorable to the plaintiffs should not be given conclusive or substantive weight when applying the doctrine of *forum non conveniens*. Reversed.

Louisville & Nashvill Railroad v. Mottley

U.S. Supreme Court, 211 U.S. 149 (1908)

FACTS

Plaintiff Husband and Wife (the Mottleys) were given a free, lifetime ticket on Defendant Louisville & Nashville Railroad in exchange for a release on prior claims against the railroad for negligence. After about 36 years of free rides, the defendant cancelled the tickets and the plaintiff brought suit in federal court. The plaintiff's complaint argued that the cancellation was based on a recent act of Congress which limited the giving away of free transportation. The circuit court granted relief to the plaintiffs without considering the jurisdictional basis. The defendant appealed.

I

Can a plaintiff argue that the defendant will raise certain defenses that arise under the constitution and obtain federal question jurisdiction?

R

A plaintiff's case must involve a federal question in order to obtain federal question jurisdiction; it can not anticipate that the defendant will raise a federal question as a possible defense if one does not already exist.

A

The plaintiff's complaint must itself raise the federal question in order to obtain jurisdiction. It is not enough that the plaintiff anticipate that the defendant will raise a federal question in a defense; even if the likelihood of the defendant doing so is great. In the instant case, the Mottleys did not raise a federal question in their complaint; they merely anticipated that the defendant would raise one in its defense. This is not an acceptable ground for federal question jurisdiction since the complaint itself must raise federal questions. Thus, jurisdiction was lacking in the instant case.

C

No. In order to obtain federal question jurisdiction, a plaintiff's case must include a federal question and may not anticipate that the defendant will raise a federal question as a possible defense. Reversed and remanded, with instruction to dismiss for lack of jurisdiction.

Redner v. Sanders

2000 WL 1161080 (S.D.N.Y. 2000)

FACTS

Plaintiff Redner sued two individual defendants and one corporate defendant, all citizens of New York, in New York federal court. In his complaint, Redner alleged that he was a United States citizen residing in France and avers that diversity exists because he "is a resident of a foreign state, while defendants are residents of the State of New York." He has not, however, established his state of citizenship. The defendants filed a motion to dismiss under Federal Rule of Civil Procedure 12(b)(1) for lack of subject matter jurisdiction.

I Can a party sufficiently establish diversity of citizenship if he is a resident of a foreign country?

R Under 28 U.S.C. §1332, a federal district court has jurisdiction over actions involving citizens of different states as well as citizens of a state and a foreign country; however, residency is not the same as citizenship.

A Under 28 U.S.C. §1332, a federal district court has jurisdiction over actions involving citizens of different states as well as citizens of a state and a foreign country. In the instant action, Redner, in his complaint, apparently seeks diversity jurisdiction by virtue of his current residency in France. Residency, however, is not synonymous with citizenship and the case does not involve an action between a citizen of a state and a citizen of a foreign country. The complaint similarly fails in its attempt to establish that the instant action involves citizens of different states. At the hearing, the plaintiff asserted that he maintains United States citizenship in California, as demonstrated by his California law license, his California driver's license from that state, and his solicitations for employment at two San Francisco law offices. However, plaintiff's factual submission is not enough to establish a California domicile, and he has yet to explain his residency in France, including where he lives, what kind of residence he has, whether he is employed there or what professional activities he carries out there. Absent such a showing, the plaintiff has failed to establish his domicile.

C Motion granted.

Saadeh v. Farouki

107 F.3d 52 (D.C. Cir. 1997)

FACTS

Plaintiff Mr. Saadeh, a Greek citizen, sued defendant Mr. Farouki, a Jordanian citizen residing in Maryland who had achieved "permanent resident" immigration status in the United States, on a defaulted loan in federal court claiming diversity jurisdiction. After the litigation was underway, Mr. Farouki became a citizen of the United States. The district court rendered a judgment for Mr. Saadeh and Mr. Farouki (defendant) appealed on the merits.

I

Is there federal diversity jurisdiction in an action involving an alien from a foreign country and another who has achieved permanent resident status in the United States?

R

There is no federal diversity jurisdiction in a suit involving an alien and one who has achieved permanent resident immigration status in the United States.

A

We do not reach the merits of the case because we find a lack of subject matter jurisdiction. Congress has never granted the district courts the full measure of diversity permitted by the Constitution and the U.S. States Supreme Court has never addressed the scope of the complete diversity rule in cases involving alien parties. However, in 1988 Congress amended the diversity statute [28 U.S.C. § 1332(a)] to provide that "an alien admitted to the United States for permanent residence shall be deemed a citizen of the State in which such alien is domiciled." Under this amendment, diversity no longer exists between a citizen of State A and an alien admitted to the United States for permanent residence who resides in State A. Read literally, however, the amendment would create diversity between Saadeh, a Greek citizen, and Farouki, one who would be deemed a resident of Maryland. Mr. Farouki subsequently becoming a U.S. citizen does not create diversity since the test is whether he was a citizen at the time the suit was filed, which he was not. Thus, the remaining question is whether Mr. Farouki (defendant) was a "citizen of the State" when the complaint was filed. A literal reading of the amendment would create an odd and possibly unconstitutional result. It would abrogate the long standing rule of diversity and create federal diversity jurisdiction over a lawsuit between two aliens, without a citizen of a state on either side of the suit. Under *Hodgson v. Bowerbank*, the U.S Supreme Court has held that the judicial power of the United States under the Diversity Clause of Article III does not extend to such an action. Therefore, we must examine the legislative history of the 1988 amendment to determine Congressional intent. The Congressional Record makes clear that the purpose of the amendment was to reduce diversity jurisdiction to relieve caseload pressures in the federal courts. Despite its plain language, the alien amendment "clearly appears to have been intended only to eliminate diversity jurisdiction between a citizen and an alien living in the same state." We do not believe the amendment was intended to create diversity jurisdiction and then expand it to situations where it did not previously exist. Since the literal language of the statue is at odds with the Congressional intent, our contrary construction is necessary to avoid constitutional difficulties.

C

Case dismissed for lack of jurisdiction.

In re Ameriquest Mortgage Co. Mortgage Lending Practices Litigation

2007 U.S. Dist. LEXIS 70805 (N.D. Ill. 2007)

FACTS

In her amended complaint, plaintiff Skanes alleges that in April 2004, she consummated a mortgage transaction with Ameriquest. Shortly before the close of the transaction, Ameriquest ordered from Co-defendant Homestead Appraisal of Rockford a property appraisal of Skanes' future home. Homestead, through its agent Trevino valued the house at $163,000. Plaintiff, however, alleges that the "true value" of the house was much less than the amount reflected in the Trevino report. The reason for this inflation, she argues, was to increase the loan amount for which she could qualify and thereby increase Ameriquest's potential profit. When the adjustable rate reset, Skanes could not refinance.

I

Does the court have subject matter jurisdiction over the plaintiffs' deformation claim pursuant to a statutory grant of supplemental jurisdiction [28 U.S.C. §1367]?

R

Supplemental jurisdiction exists when a state-law claim shares "a common nucleus of operative fact" with a federal claim and jurisdiction would further judicial economy, convenience and fairness.

A

28 U.S.C. §1367 provides that any action in which we already have jurisdiction over some federal claim, we also have supplemental jurisdiction over state claims "that are so related to claims in the action within such original jurisdictional that they form part of the same case or controversy under Article II of the Constitution ..." A loose factual connection may be sufficient to confer supplemental jurisdiction so long as those facts are both common and operative. Here Skanes explicitly connected here federal and state claims such that we cannot now conclude that her state claim could be dismissed or resolved without affecting her TILA (Truth in Lending Act) (i.e. federal) claim. Skanes now seeks a judgment to void her allegedly overstated mortgage. In doing so, she expressly links here TILA prayer for relief to her state claims. We find this connection operative: if we dismiss Counts II and III, we may be unable to grant the full measure of Relief she seeks in Claim I. Because we cannot conclude that the resolution of one of her state claims will have no effect on the resolution of her federal claims, we cannot deny our supplemental jurisdiction here.

C

See above.

Szendrey-Ramos v. First Bancorp

2007 U.S. Dist. LEXIS 74896 (D.P.R. 2007)

FACTS

Plaintiff Carmen Szendrey-Ramos was general counsel for defendant First Bancorp in Puerto Rico. When an outside law firm sent Szendrey a report alleging possible ethical and legal violations by bank officials, Szendrey conducted an investigation. Szendrey (D) found that there were some violations of the bank's code of ethics. The bank fired Szendrey, blaming her for some of the events she had investigated. She sued under the federal Title VII of the 1964 Civil Rights Act for discrimination and retaliation, and under Puerto Rico law for wrongful discharge, defamation, tortuous interference with contract, and violations of the Puerto Rico constitution.

I

May a court may decline to exercise supplemental jurisdiction where (1) the state law claims raise complex or novel issues, or (2) the state law claims substantially predominate over the federal claim?

R

A court may decline to exercise supplemental jurisdiction where (1) the state law claims raise complex or novel issues, or (2) the state law claims substantially predominate over the federal claim

A

Yes. A court may decline to exercise supplemental jurisdiction where (1) the state law claims raise complex or novel issues, or (2) the state law claims substantially predominate over the federal claim. Here, the state law claims exceed the federal claims in number and scope. Some of the state claims mimic the federal claims, but most--including wrongful discharge, tortious interference with contracts, and defamation--are distinct and have their own elements of proof, which is not necessary to establish the Title VII claims. The predominance of the state claims over the federal claims is enough to decline to exercise supplemental jurisdiction. But Puerto Rican law claims require a more probing analysis of Szendrey's (P) performance as general counsel, and any shortcomings she may have had, and this leads to another reason for declining to exercise supplemental jurisdiction, which is the presence of complex or novel issues of state law. The interpretation of the relevant Puerto Rico laws is usually the province of the Puerto Rico Supreme Court. The laws at issue in this case are silent on the issue of a lawyer's claim against her former client, and the possibility of divulging confidential information in order to pursue such a claim, and Puerto Rico courts have not yet addressed the issue. Therefore, the Puerto Rico law claims will be dismissed without prejudice, so they may be re-filed in Puerto Rico courts.

C

Accordingly, the Puerto Rico law claims will be dismissed without prejudice, so plaintiffs may re-file them in Puerto Rico courts.

Caterpillar Inc. v. Lewis

U.S. Supreme Court, 519 U.S. 61 (1996)

FACTS

Respondent Lewis, a Kentucky resident, commenced this civil action in Kentucky state court after sustaining personal injuries while operating a bulldozer. Asserting state-law claims, Lewis named as defendants both the manufacturer of the bulldozer-petitioner Caterpillar Inc., a Delaware corporation with its principal place of business in Illinois-and the company that serviced the bulldozer-Whayne Supply Company, a Kentucky corporation with its principal place of business in Kentucky. Liberty Mutual Insurance Group, a Massachusetts corporation with its principal place of business in that State, intervened as a plaintiff, asserting subrogation claims against both Caterpillar and Whayne Supply for workers' compensation benefits Liberty Mutual had paid to Lewis on behalf of his employer. Shortly after learning of a settlement agreement between Lewis and Whayne Supply, Caterpillar filed a notice of removal in Federal District Court, grounding federal jurisdiction on diversity of citizenship, see 28 U. S. C. Section(s) 1332. The notice explained that the case was non-removable at the lawsuit's start: Complete diversity was absent then because plaintiff Lewis and defendant Whayne Supply shared Kentucky citizenship. Caterpillar assumed that the settlement agreement between these two parties would result in Whayne Supply's dismissal from the lawsuit, yielding complete diversity and rendering the case removable. Lewis promptly moved to remand the case to state court, asserting that diversity was defeated by Whayne Supply's continuing presence as a defendant due to Liberty Mutual's subrogation claim against it. The District Court denied the motion, erroneously concluding that diversity had become complete. Before trial, however, Liberty Mutual's subrogation claim against Whayne Supply was settled, and that defendant was dismissed as a party. Complete diversity thereafter existed. The case proceeded to trial, jury verdict, and judgment for Caterpillar. The Sixth Circuit vacated the judgment, concluding that, absent complete diversity at the time of removal, the District Court lacked subject-matter jurisdiction.

I

Is a district court's error in failing to remand a case which has been improperly removed fatal to the ensuing adjudication if federal jurisdictional requirements are met at the time judgment is entered?

R

A district court's error in failing to remand a case improperly removed is not fatal to the ensuing adjudication if federal jurisdictional requirements are met at the time judgment is entered.

A

The general-diversity statute, Section(s) 1332(a), authorizes federal court jurisdiction over cases in which the citizenship of each plaintiff is diverse from the citizenship of each defendant. When a plaintiff files a state-court civil action over which the federal district courts would have original jurisdiction based on diversity of citizenship, the defendant or defendants may remove the action to federal court, Section(s) 1441(a), provided that no defendant "is a citizen of the State in which such action is brought," Section(s) 1441(b). In a case not originally removable from state court, a defendant who receives a pleading or other paper indicating the post-commencement satisfaction of federal jurisdictional requirements - e.g., by reason of a non-diverse party's dismissal-may remove the case to federal court within 30 days. Section(s) 1446(b). No case, however, may be removed based on diversity "more than 1 year after commencement of the action." Once a defendant has filed a notice of removal in the federal court, a plaintiff objecting to removal "on the basis of any defect in removal procedure" may, within 30 days, file a motion to remand the case to state court. Section(s) 1447(c). This 30-day limit does not apply, however, to jurisdictional defects: "If at any time before final judgment it appears that the district court lacks subject matter Jurisdiction, the case shall be remanded." *American Fire & Casualty Co. v. Finn* and *Grubbs v. General Elec. Credit Corp.* are key cases in point and tend in Caterpillar's favor. Each suggests that the existence of subject-matter jurisdiction at time of judgment may shield a judgment against later jurisdictional attack despite an improper removal. However, neither decision resolves dispositively a controversy of the kind here at issue, for neither involved a plaintiff who moved promptly, but unsuccessfully, to remand a case improperly removed from state court to federal court, and then challenged on appeal a judgment entered by the federal court. Caterpillar moves too quickly in claiming that elimination of the jurisdictional defect before trial also cured a statutory flaw-Caterpillar's failure to meet the Section(s) 1441(a) requirement that the case be fit for federal adjudication at the time the removal petition was filed. By timely moving for remand, Lewis did all that was necessary to preserve his objection to removal. Having preserved his objection, Lewis urges that ultimate satisfaction of the subject-matter jurisdiction requirement ought not swallow up antecedent statutory violations. Lewis' arguments in support of this position are hardly meritless, but they run up against an overriding consideration. Once a diversity case has been tried in federal court, with rules of decision supplied by state law under the regime of *Erie R. Co. v. Tompkins* considerations of finality, efficiency, and economy become overwhelming. This view is in harmony with a main theme of the removal scheme devised by Congress, which calls for expeditious superintendence by district courts. In this case, no jurisdictional defect lingered through judgment in the District Court. To wipe out the adjudication post-judgment, and return to state court a case now satisfying all federal jurisdictional requirements, would impose an exorbitant cost on our dual court system, a cost incompatible with the fair and unprotracted administration of justice. Lewis' prediction that rejection of his petition will provide state-court defendants with an enormous incentive to attempt unlawful removals rests on an assumption this Court does not indulge-that federal district courts generally will not comprehend, or will balk at applying, the removal rules Congress has prescribed. This Court is satisfied that the well-advised defendant will foresee the likely outcome of an unwarranted removal-a swift, and non-reviewable remand order, see whose authority has been improperly invoked.

C

Reversed and remanded.

Erie Railroad v. Tompkins

U.S. Supreme Court, 304 U.S. 64 (1938)

FACTS

Harry Tompkins (plaintiff) was struck by an object which extended from a moving train owned by the Erie Railroad (defendant). This incident occurred while he was walking along the railroad's foot path in Pennsylvania adjacent to the tracks. Plaintiff sued Defendant Erie Railroad for negligence based on diversity of jurisdiction in a New York federal District Court. Plaintiff Tompkins argued that the railroad owed a duty of care to ordinary pedestrians and that the federal courts must follow statutory law according to *Swift*. However, Erie Railroad argued that Pennsylvania common law should apply as the plaintiff was a trespasser to whom the defendant only owed a duty to avoid wanton negligence. The District Court and the Court of Appeals agreed with Tompkins (plaintiff) and applied general law, awarding Tompkins $30,000 in damages. The Supreme Court of the United States granted certiorari.

I

Is a federal court required to apply federal common law (in the absence of a state statute)?

R

Federal courts are required to apply the substantive common law of the state in which they sit (Erie Doctrine).

A

Congress has no power to declare substantive rules of common law applicable to state actions. Hence, Congress could not have delegated this power to the federal courts via §34 as there is no federal general common law. Therefore, we hold *Swift* unconstitutional for the following reasons: *Swift* was based on the misinterpretation of the Rules of Decision Act, §34, and, as such, it has led to discrimination against parties sued in federal court via diversity jurisdiction. Under *Swift*, a plaintiff of diverse citizenship could choose whether state or federal law would apply by selecting either the state forum or the federal forum. This application of *Swift* prevented uniformity of law throughout the land. Therefore, we hold that the *Swift* interpretation of §34 is unconstitutional, although §34 itself is not.

C

No. Federal courts are required to apply the substantive common law of the state in which they sit. Reversed and remanded.

Guaranty Trust Co. v. York

U.S. Supreme Court, 326 U.S. 99 (1945)

FACTS

The plaintiff sued the defendant for an alleged breach of fiduciary duty owed to him as it related to a trust. York (plaintiff) sued Guaranty Trust Co. (defendant), a trustee, for allegedly failing to protect his interest in a trust. The plaintiff brought the action in federal court based on diversity of citizenship, claiming allegations of fraud and misrepresentation which would have been barred if it were brought in state court because of the state's statute of limitations. Defendant Guaranty Trust argued that the state statute of limitations should apply to the present action in federal court. The Circuit Court of Appeals held that the federal District Court was not required to apply the state statute of limitations when hearing a suit brought in equity. The Supreme Court of the United States granted certiorari.

I

Must a federal court apply a state's statute of limitations in a diversity action?

R

A federal court MUST apply a state statute; that is, apply a state's procedural rules (in this case the state statute of limitations) if those rules have a substantial impact on the litigation.

A

Federal courts with diversity jurisdiction must apply state statutes of limitations if those statutes would have a "substantial impact" on the litigation. Pursuant to the Erie Doctrine, federal courts must apply state substantive common law. State law is substantive if it would have a substantial effect on the eventual outcome of the case and statutes of limitation can in fact be substantive within the bounds of the Erie Doctrine. The intent of *Erie* was to ensure that federal courts exercising diversity jurisdiction arrive at the same results that a state court would have in the same situation.

C

Yes. A federal court must apply a state statute; that is, apply state procedural rules, in this case the state statute of limitations, if those rules have a substantial impact on the litigation. Reversed.

Byrd v. Blue Ridge Rural Electric Cooperative

U.S. Supreme Court, 356 U.S. 525 (1958)

FACTS

The plaintiff sued the defendant for negligence relating to an accident sustained during his temporary employment. Byrd (plaintiff) was a lineman for a construction company that contracted with the Blue Ridge Electric Cooperative (defendant). Blue Ridge was an electric company. After Plaintiff Byrd was injured connecting power lines, he sued Blue Ridge in South Carolina federal court based on diversity of citizenship. Defendant Blue Ridge contended that, pursuant to South Carolina's Workmen's Compensation Act, Byrd was required to bring a Workmen's Compensation action and not the civil action he filed. Consequently, a factual dispute arose as to whether the plaintiff should be considered a statutory employee for the purposes of Workmen's Compensation or not. In South Carolina, such a determination can only be made by the trial judge. However, federal procedural rules would require the issue to go to a jury. The Court of Appeals for the Fourth Circuit reversed a jury verdict in favor of Plaintiff Byrd and he obtained certiorari by the Supreme Court of the United States.

I

Must federal courts always apply state procedural rules that are potentially outcome determinative?

R

If federal policy, in enacting the rules, outweighs state policy, federal courts may apply federal rules even if the state rules are outcome determinative.

A

A balancing test should be used weighing state policies behind the rule against countervailing federal policies. Consistent with the Erie Doctrine, state procedural rules which affect the substantive outcome of a suit should be applied if they are an integral part of some substantive right. In the instant case, South Carolina's common law required the determination of a person's status as a statutory employee to be determined by the judge. However, South Carolina's rational for the rule was not to further some substantive state policy and was not bound up with the definition of the rights and obligations of the parties. It was simply a procedural practice established by the South Carolina Supreme Court. Thus, the balance shifts in favor of the federal policy, which would allow the issue to go to a jury. Because (1) the application of the common law of South Carolina would deprive Byrd of a jury trial; and (2) South Carolina has not advanced any critical policy goals which would justify the denial of Byrd's fundamental rights (Seventh Amendment right to a jury), the issue should go to a jury.

C

No. If federal policy outweighs state policy in enacting the rules, federal courts may apply federal rules even if the state rules are outcome determinative. Reversed and remanded.

Hanna v. Plumer

U.S. Supreme Court, 380 U.S. 460 (1965)

FACTS

Hanna (plaintiff) was injured in an automobile accident with Louise Plumer Osgood (defendant), who has since died. Plaintiff Hanna filed suit in federal District Court in Massachusetts based on diversity of citizenship. Service of process was made on the defendant's executor by leaving copies of the summons and complaint with the executor's wife. The defendant's executor claimed the service was improper, according to Rule 4(d)(1), because it did not conform to Massachusetts statutory law. This law required personal service on the executor himself. The District Court granted the defendant's motion for summary judgment pursuant to *York* (a federal court must apply outcome determinative state law) and the Court of Appeals for the First Circuit Affirmed.

I

In a conflict between a state law (which is outcome determinative) and a Federal Rule of Civil Procedure, which law controls?

R

The Federal Rules of Civil Procedure trump state laws which are outcome determinative within the scope of the Rules Enabling Act.

A

The Federal Rules of Civil Procedure trump state laws which are outcome determinative within the scope of the Rules Enabling Act. The Rules Enabling Act, 28 U.S.C. §2072, grants the Supreme Court the authority to prescribe rules of procedure for federal District Courts. Rule 4(d)(1) was enacted within the limits of the Rules Enabling Act since it regulated the procedures of the District Courts. Therefore, if there are no conflicting state procedures, Rule 4(d)(1) would clearly control and service of process would have been proper in the case at hand. However, the argument is defective. First off, the instant case is fundamentally different from the situations of *Erie* and *York*, neither of which dealt with a Federal Rule of Civil Procedure conflicting with a state law. Moreover, the outcome determination analysis was never intended to be a "cure all". That is, where a conflict exists between a state law and a federal law, the state law should only be applied in reference to the two primary objectives of the Erie Doctrine: (1) discouragement of forum shopping and (2) the avoidance of inequitable administration.

C

No. The Federal Rules of Civil Procedure trump state laws which are outcome determinative within the scope of the Rules Enabling Act. Judgment reversed.

Semtek Intl. Inc. v. Lockheed Martin Corp.

U.S. Supreme Court, 531 U.S. 497 (2001)

FACTS

Respondent removed petitioner's California state-court suit to a California Federal District Court based on diversity of citizenship, and successfully moved to dismiss the case "on the merits" as barred by California's statute of limitations. Petitioner then brought suit in a Maryland Circuit Court, alleging the same causes of action, which were not time barred under Maryland's statute of limitations. That court dismissed the case on the ground of res judicata. In affirming, the Maryland Court of Special Appeals held that, regardless of whether California would have accorded claim-preclusive effect to a statute-of-limitations dismissal by one of its own courts, the California federal court's dismissal barred the Maryland complaint because the res judicata effect of federal diversity judgments is prescribed by federal law, under which the earlier dismissal was on the merits and claim-preclusive. The U.S. Supreme Court granted review.

I Should federal courts apply the procedural law of the forum state in which they sit?

R Federal courts should apply the procedural law of the forum state in which they sit.

A Because the claim-preclusive effect of a federal court's dismissal "upon the merits" of a diversity action on state statute-of-limitations grounds is governed by a federal rule, which in turn (in diversity cases) incorporates the claim-preclusion law that would be applied by state courts in the State in which the federal court sits, the Maryland Court of Special Appeals erred in holding that the California federal court's dismissal "upon the merits" necessarily precluded the Maryland state-court action. *Dupasseur* v. *Rochereau* held that the res judicata effect of a federal diversity judgment "is such as would belong to judgments of the State courts rendered under similar circumstances." That case is not dispositive here, however, because it was decided under the Conformity Act of 1872, which required federal courts to apply the procedural law of the forum State in non-equity cases. Neither is claim-preclusive effect demanded by Rule 41(b)--which provides that, unless the court "otherwise specifies," an involuntary dismissal, other than a dismissal for lack of jurisdiction, improper venue, or failure to join a party under Rule 19, "operates as an adjudication upon the merits." Although the original connotation of a judgment "on the merits" was one that passes directly on the substance of a claim (which would be claim-preclusive), the meaning of the term has undergone change, and does not necessarily designate a judgment effecting claim preclusion. There are a number of reasons for believing it does not bear that meaning in Rule 41(b). It would be peculiar to announce a federally prescribed rule on claim preclusion in a default rule for determining a dismissal's import, or to find a rule governing the effect to be accorded federal judgments by other courts ensconced in rules governing the internal procedures of the rendering court itself. Moreover, as so interpreted, the Rule would in many cases violate the federalism principle of *Erie R. Co.* v. *Tompkins,* by engendering substantial variations in outcomes between state and federal litigation which would likely influence forum choice, *Hanna* v. *Plumer*. Finally, this Court has never relied upon the Rule when recognizing the claim-preclusive effect of federal judgments in federal-question cases. Rule 41(a) makes clear that "an adjudication upon the merits" in Rule 41(b) is the opposite of a dismissal without prejudice--that is, it is a dismissal that prevents refiling of the claim in the same court. That is undoubtedly a necessary condition, but not a sufficient one, for claim-preclusive effect in other courts. Federal common law governs the claim-preclusive effect of a dismissal by a federal court sitting in diversity, and it is up to this Court to determine the appropriate federal rule. Since in diversity cases state, rather than federal, substantive law is at issue, there is no need for a uniform federal rule; and nationwide uniformity is better served by having the same claim-preclusive rule (the state rule) apply whether the dismissal has been ordered by a state or a federal court. Any other rule would produce the sort of forum shopping and inequitable administration of the laws that *Erie* seeks to avoid. While the federal reference to state law will not obtain in situations in which the state law is incompatible with federal interests, no such conflict exists here.

C

Reversed and remanded.

State Farm Mutual Insur. Co. v. Campbell

U.S. Supreme Court, 123 S. Ct. 1513 (2003)

FACTS

Although investigators and witnesses concluded that Curtis Campbell caused an accident in which one person was killed and another permanently disabled, his insurer, petitioner State Farm Mutual Automobile Insurance Company (State Farm), contested liability, declined to settle the ensuing claims for the $50,000 policy limit, ignored its own investigators' advice, and took the case to trial, assuring Campbell and his wife that they had no liability for the accident, that State Farm would represent their interests, and that they did not need separate counsel. In fact, a Utah jury returned a judgment for over three times the policy limit, and State Farm refused to appeal. The Utah Supreme Court denied Campbell's own appeal, and State Farm paid the entire judgment. The Campbells then sued State Farm for bad faith, fraud, and intentional infliction of emotional distress. The trial court's initial ruling granting State Farm summary judgment was reversed on appeal. On remand, the court denied State Farm's motion to exclude evidence of dissimilar out-of-state conduct. In the first phase of a bifurcated trial, the jury found unreasonable State Farm's decision not to settle. Before the second phase, this Court refused, in *BMW of North America, Inc.* v. *Gore,* to sustain a $2 million punitive damages award which accompanied a $4,000 compensatory damages award. The trial court denied State Farm's renewed motion to exclude dissimilar out-of-state conduct evidence. In the second phase, which addressed, *inter alia,* compensatory and punitive damages, evidence was introduced that pertained to State Farm's business practices in numerous States but bore no relation to the type of claims underlying the Campbells' complaint. The jury awarded the Campbells $2.6 million in compensatory damages and $145 million in punitive damages, which the trial court reduced to $1 million and $25 million respectively. Applying *Gore,* the Utah Supreme Court reinstated the $145 million punitive damages award.

I

When a punitive damages award so greatly exceeds the award for full compensatory damages, is the 14th Amendment violated?

R

A punitive damages award of $145 million, where full compensatory damages are $1 million, is excessive and violates the Due Process Clause of the Fourteenth Amendment

A

A punitive damages award of $145 million, where full compensatory damages are $1 million, is excessive and violates the Due Process Clause of the Fourteenth Amendment. Compensatory damages are intended to redress a plaintiff's concrete loss, while punitive damages are aimed at the different purposes of deterrence and retribution. The Due Process Clause prohibits the imposition of grossly excessive or arbitrary punishments on a tortfeasor. Punitive damages awards serve the same purpose as criminal penalties. However, because civil defendants are not accorded the protections afforded criminal defendants, punitive damages pose an acute danger of arbitrary deprivation of property, which is heightened when the decisionmaker is presented with evidence having little bearing on the amount that should be awarded. Thus, this Court has instructed courts reviewing punitive damages to consider (1) the degree of reprehensibility of the defendant's misconduct, (2) the disparity between the actual or potential harm suffered by the plaintiff and the punitive damages award, and (3) the difference between the punitive damages awarded by the jury and the civil penalties authorized or imposed in comparable cases. A trial court's application of these guideposts is subject to *de novo* review. Under *Gore*'s guideposts, this case is neither close nor difficult. To determine a defendant's reprehensibility--the most important indicium of a punitive damages award's reasonableness--a court must consider whether: the harm was physical rather than economic; the tortious conduct evinced an indifference to or a reckless disregard of the health or safety of others; the conduct involved repeated actions or was an isolated incident; and the harm resulted from intentional malice, trickery, or deceit, or mere accident. It should be presumed that a plaintiff has been made whole by compensatory damages, so punitive damages should be awarded only if the defendant's culpability is so reprehensible to warrant the imposition of further sanctions to achieve punishment or deterrence. In this case, State Farm's handling of the claims against the Campbells merits no praise, but a more modest punishment could have satisfied the State's legitimate objectives. Instead, this case was used as a platform to expose, and punish, the perceived deficiencies of State Farm's operations throughout the country. However, a State cannot punish a defendant for conduct that may have been lawful where it occurred, *id.,* at 572. Nor does the State have a legitimate concern in imposing punitive damages to punish a defendant for unlawful acts committed outside of its jurisdiction. The Campbells argue that such evidence was used merely to demonstrate, generally, State Farm's motives against its insured. Lawful out-of-state conduct may be probative when it demonstrates the deliberateness and culpability of the defendant's action in the State where it is tortious, but that conduct must have a nexus to the specific harm suffered by the plaintiff. More fundamentally, in relying on such evidence, the Utah courts awarded punitive damages to punish and deter conduct that bore no relation to the Campbells' harm. Due process does not permit courts to adjudicate the merits of other parties' hypothetical claims under the guise of the reprehensibility analysis. Punishment on these bases creates the possibility of multiple punitive damages awards for the same conduct, for nonparties are not normally bound by another plaintiff's judgment. For the same reasons, the Utah Supreme Court's decision cannot be justified on the grounds that State Farm was a recidivist. To justify punishment based upon recidivism, courts must ensure the conduct in question replicates the prior transgressions. There is scant evidence of repeated misconduct of the sort that injured the Campbells, and a review of the decisions below does not convince this Court that State Farm was only punished for its actions toward the Campbells. Because the Campbells have shown no conduct similar to that which harmed them, the only relevant conduct to the reprehensibility analysis is that which harmed them. With regard to the second *Gore* guidepost, the Court has been reluctant to identify concrete constitutional limits on the ratio between harm, or potential harm, to the plaintiff and the punitive damages award; but, in practice, few awards exceeding a single-digit ratio between punitive and compensatory damages will satisfy due process. Single-digit multipliers are more likely to comport with due process, while still achieving the State's deterrence and retribution goals, than are awards with 145-to-1 ratios, as in this case. Because there are no rigid benchmarks, ratios greater than those that this Court has previously upheld may comport with due process where a particularly egregious act has resulted in only a small amount of economic damages, but when compensatory damages are substantial, then an even lesser ratio can reach the outermost limit of the due process guarantee. Here, there is a presumption against an award with a 145-to-1 ratio; the $1 million compensatory award for a year and a half of emotional distress was substantial; and the distress caused by outrage and humiliation the Campbells suffered is likely a component of both the compensatory and punitive damages awards. The Utah Supreme Court sought to justify the massive award based on premises bearing no relation to the award's reasonableness or proportionality to the harm. The Court need not dwell on the third guidepost. The most relevant civil sanction under Utah state law for the wrong done to the Campbells appears to be a $10,000 fine for an act of grand fraud, which is dwarfed by the $145 million punitive damages award. The Utah Supreme Court's references to a broad fraudulent scheme drawn from out-of-state and dissimilar conduct evidence were insufficient to justify this amount. Applying *Gore*'s guideposts to the facts here, especially in light of the substantial compensatory damages award, likely would justify a punitive damages award at or near the compensatory damages amount. The Utah courts should resolve in the first instance the proper punitive damages calculation under the principles discussed here.

C

Reversed and remanded.

Sigma Chemical Co. v. Harris

605 F. Supp 1253 (E.D. Mo. 1985)

FACTS

Sigma Chemical Co. (plaintiff) is a Missouri corporation that sells chemicals used in research, production, and analysis. At the heart of its business is matching the right supplier with one or more of its products. Sigma's knowledge of which supplier resells a particular chemical of a certain quality that satisfied a particular purpose at the right price is a trade secret. Foster Harris went to work for Sigma in 1979, after signing an employment/confidentiality covenant/agreement that he would not work for a competitor for two years after leaving Sigma and that he would never disclose confidential information acquired from Sigma. In 1983, Harris (defendant) went to work for ICN, one of Sigma's five major competitors. Sigma sought to enjoin Harris from working for ICN.

I

Does a company's interest in keeping a trade secret sufficiently outweigh a former employee's interest in seeking employment elsewhere such that the former will be entitled to permanent injunctive relief against the latter?

R

The determination whether to issue an injunction involves a balancing of the interests of the parties who might be affected by the court's decision.

A

The interest at issue here are no insignificant: Sigma has a legitimate interest in protecting its trade secrets and Harris has a legitimate interest in being able to seek employment elsewhere. The restrictive covenant at issue here is valid and necessary to protect Sigma's legitimate interest in keeping a trade secret. It is also reasonable in both temporal and geographic scope. The determination whether to issue an injunction involves a balancing of the interests of the parties who might be affected by the Court's decision. Moreover, the "main prerequisite to obtaining injunctive relief is a finding that the plaintiff is being threatened by some injury for which he has no adequate legal remedy." First, it is clear that Harris is violating or would violate the terms of the covenant. Harris is contributing his knowledge to a service or product which is in competition with the interests/services/products of Sigma. Harris is in a position that makes it likely he will use or disclose trade secret information that Harris learned from Sigma's product files. Under these circumstances there is a strong threat of irreparable harm to Sigma. On the other hand, Harris also faces substantial harm. He will be prevented from working for ICN for two years and likely will forever be prevented from using his knowledge of Sigma's trade secrets. However, the potential harm to Harris is diminished by the fact that other former Sigma employees have obtained employment with companies not in competition with Sigma. Therefore, we decide, after a careful examination of the interests of both parties, that a balancing of the equities do not favor Harris because (1) he was aware of the restrictions when he took employment with Sigma and (2) he took a knowing and calculated risk by deciding to violate the contract. On balance, the threat to Sigma outweighs the detriment to Harris. Thus, it is ordered that Harris be enjoined from rendering services to ICN as a purchasing agent involved in the purchase of products also sold by Sigma for a period of two years; and using or disclosing any trade secret that is the property of Sigma and which Harris acquired by reason of his employment with Sigma. Accordingly, Sigma is entitled to permanent injunctive relief.

C

See above.

Evans v. Jeff D.

U.S. Supreme Court, 475 U.S. 717 (1986)

FACTS

The Civil Rights Attorney's Fees Awards Act of 1976 (Fees Act) provides that "the court, in its discretion, may allow the prevailing party . . . a reasonable attorney's fee" in enumerated civil rights actions. Respondents brought a class action against petitioners (the Governor and other public officials of Idaho responsible for the education and treatment of mentally handicapped children) in Federal District Court on behalf of children who have been or will be placed in petitioners' care. It was alleged that deficiencies in both the educational programs and health care services provided respondents violated the Federal and State Constitutions and various federal and state statutes. Injunctive relief and an award of costs and attorney's fees were sought. Ultimately, the District Court approved a settlement granting the injunctive relief sought conditional on respondents' waiver of any claim for attorney's fees. The Court of Appeals invalidated the fee waiver, left standing the remainder of the settlement, and remanded to the District Court to determine what attorney's fees were reasonable, holding that the historical background of Federal Rule of Civil Procedure 23(e), which gives a district court power to approve settlements of class actions, and of the Fees Act, compelled the conclusion that a stipulated waiver of attorney's fees obtained solely as a condition for obtaining relief for the class should not be accepted by the court.

I

Does a district court have the power to waive attorneys' fees?

R

The District Court had the power, in its discretion, to approve the waiver of attorney's fees.

A

The District Court had the power, in its discretion, to approve the waiver of attorney's fees. The language of the Fees Act, as well as its legislative history, indicates that Congress bestowed on the "prevailing party" a statutory eligibility for a discretionary award of attorney's fees in specified civil rights actions. Neither the statute nor the legislative history suggests that Congress intended to forbid all waivers of attorney's fees. Congress neither bestowed fee awards upon attorneys nor rendered them non-waivable or nonnegotiable; instead, it added them to the remedies available to combat civil rights violations, a goal not invariably inconsistent with conditioning settlement on the merits on a waiver of statutory attorney's fees. A general proscription against waiver of attorney's fees in exchange for a settlement on the merits would itself impede vindication of civil rights, at least in some cases, by reducing the attractiveness of settlement. It is not implausible to anticipate that parties to a significant number of civil rights cases would refuse to settle if liability for attorney's fees remained open, thereby forcing more cases to trial, unnecessarily burdening the judicial system, and disserving civil rights litigants. The

District Court did not abuse its discretion in approving a waiver of attorney's fees that secured broad injunctive relief greater than that which respondents could reasonably have expected to achieve at trial. There is nothing in the record to indicate that Idaho has adopted a statute, policy, or practice insisting on a fee waiver as a condition of settlement in civil rights litigation in conflict with the Fees Act. Nor does the record indicate that petitioners' request to waive fees was a vindictive effort to deter attorneys from representing plaintiffs in civil rights suits against Idaho.

C

Reversed.

Buckhannon Board and Care Home Inc. v. West Virginia Dept. of Health and Human Resources

U.S. Supreme Court, 532 U.S. 598 (2001)

FACTS

Buckhannon Board and Care Home, Inc., which operates assisted living residences, failed an inspection by the West Virginia fire marshal's office because some residents were incapable of "self-preservation" as defined by state law. After receiving orders to close its facilities, Buckhannon and others (hereinafter petitioners) brought suit in Federal District Court against the State and state agencies and officials (hereinafter respondents), seeking declaratory and injunctive relief that the "self-preservation" requirement violated the Fair Housing Amendments Act of 1988 (FHAA) and the Americans with Disabilities Act of 1990 (ADA). Respondents agreed to stay the orders pending the case's resolution. The state legislature then eliminated the "self-preservation" requirement, and the District Court granted respondents' motion to dismiss the case as moot. Petitioners requested attorney's fees as the "prevailing party" under the FHAA and ADA, basing their entitlement on the "catalyst theory," which posits that a plaintiff is a "prevailing party" if it achieves the desired result because the lawsuit brought about a voluntary change in the defendant's conduct. As the Fourth Circuit had previously rejected the "catalyst theory," the District Court denied the motion, and the Fourth Circuit affirmed.

I

Is the "catalyst theory" a permissible basis for the award of attorney's fees under the FHAA and ADA?

R

The "catalyst theory" is not a permissible basis for the award of attorney's fees under the FHAA and ADA.

A

The "catalyst theory" is not a permissible basis for the award of attorney's fees under the FHAA and ADA. Under the "American Rule," parties are ordinarily required to bear their own attorney's fees, and courts follow a general practice of not awarding fees to a prevailing party absent explicit statutory authority, *Key Tronic Corp.* v. *United States*. Congress has employed the legal term of art "prevailing party" in numerous statutes authorizing awards of attorney's fees. A "prevailing party" is one who has been awarded some relief by a court. Both judgments on the merits and court-ordered consent decrees create a material alteration of the parties' legal relationship and thus permit an award. The "catalyst theory," however, allows an award where there is no judicially sanctioned change in the parties' legal relationship. A defendant's voluntary change in conduct, although perhaps accomplishing what the plaintiff sought to achieve by the lawsuit, lacks the necessary judicial *imprimatur* on the change. The legislative history cited by petitioners is at best ambiguous as to the availability of the "catalyst theory"; and, particularly in view of the

---

"American Rule," such history is clearly insufficient to alter the clear meaning of "prevailing party" in the fee-shifting statutes. Given this meaning, this Court need not determine which way petitioners' various policy arguments cut.

C

Affirmed.

William Inglis & Son Baking Co. v. ITT Continental Baking Co.

526 F.2d 86 (9th Cir. 1976)

FACTS

Plaintiff William Inglis & Sons Baking Co. and four other wholesale baking companies filed an antitrust action against defendant ITT Continental Baking Co. and four other defendants. Inglis moved for a preliminary injunction to prevent ITT's below-cost pricing of their "private label" bread products. "Private label" bread products are produced by the wholesale baker for sale under the retail grocer's own label rather than under a nationally-advertised brand label. As one of their defenses to this allegation, ITT claimed that its pricing scheme was a good faith effort to meet competition. The District Court held a hearing and denied Inglis' motion because it had "serious reservations about [Inglis'] probability of success on the merits." Furthermore, even assuming a prima facie violation under the applicable statutes, the court found that ITT had adequately negated such a violation by providing a valid defense. The Court of Appeals vacated the decision and remanded for a new hearing.

I Is it necessary that party moving for a preliminary injunction show that there is a reasonable certainty the party will succeed on the merits?

R A party moving for a preliminary injunction meets his burden if he shows that there is a combination of probable success and the possibility of irreparable injury or that serious questions are raised and the balance of the hardships tips sharply in its favor.

A The district court stated that a plaintiff is entitled to a preliminary injunction only if: (1) the plaintiff will suffer irreparable injury if relief is not granted; (2) the plaintiff will probably prevail on the merits; (3) in balancing the equities, the defendants will not be harmed more than plaintiff is helped by the injunction; and (4) granting the injunction is in the public interest. The court denied the injunction because it held serious doubts as to whether plaintiff would probably succeed on the merits. Our review of the grant or denial of a preliminary injunction issued by a lower court is subject to reversal by us only if it was based on an erroneous legal premise, or if the court abused its discretion. That was not the case here. We are unable to conclude that the District Court abused its discretion in its conclusion that the plaintiff failed to satisfy the standard applied by the court. However, there is an alternate test the district court failed to consider and did not apply. That test, first enunciated by the 2nd Circuit in *Charlie's Girls Inc. v. Revlon Inc.*, states that "a party moving for a preliminary injunction meets his burden if he shows that there is a combination of probable success and the possibility of irreparable injury or that serious questions are raised and the balance of the hardships tips sharply in his favor." Since the District Court did not consider whether the injunction should be issued under this alternate standard, we remand the question for further consideration. We, however, intimate no position as to whether the preliminary injunction should be issued.

C

Reversed.

Fuentes v. Shevin

U.S. Supreme Court, 407 U.S. 67 (1972)

FACTS

This case presents two separate appellate rulings regarding the constitutionality of replevin statutes; one in Florida and one in Pennsylvania. The facts presented are for one of the two appellate rulings. The Supreme Court's determination follows for both. Plaintiff Margarita Fuentes had purchased a stove and stereo under a sales contract from supplier Firestone Rubber Company (Firestone). Firestone was to retain title to the merchandise until the plaintiff made all of her required payments. After a dispute arose between the parties, Firestone initiated a claim in small claims court for repossession of the goods claiming the plaintiff refused to make the payments. Firestone simultaneously obtained a writ of replevin (action allowing the title holder to repossess goods). Afterward, plaintiff initiated the present action in federal District Court challenging the constitutionality of Florida's replevin statute. The District Court rejected the constitutional claims and upheld the constitutionality of the statute. The Supreme Court of the United States granted certiorari.

I

Must notice and opportunity to be heard BEFORE the deprivation of a property interest?

R

Notice and opportunity must be given before the deprivation of a property interest in order to comply with the requirements of due process, absent extraordinary circumstances.

A

Notice and opportunity must be given before the deprivation of a property interest in order to comply with the requirements of due process, absent extraordinary circumstances. The notice and opportunity must be granted at a consequential time; that is, at a time when the deprivation can still be reversed. Moreover, pursuant to both statutes, the creditor must post a bond such that he may be forced to pay for any wrongful possession if in fact the possession was wrong as determined by the court. However, extraordinary circumstances such as those which support a governmental interest or those in the general public interest do give rise to deprivation of property WITHOUT notice and an opportunity to be heard. However, in those situations, the statute must be narrowly drawn. **DISSENT:** The majority wrongfully ignores the creditor's interest in preventing further use and/or destruction of the property to be seized.

C

Yes. Notice and opportunity must be given prior the deprivation of a property interest in order to comply with the requirements of due process absent extraordinary circumstances. Vacated and Remanded.

Haddle v. Garrison (S.D. Ga. 1996)

Unpublished Opinion. Docket No. 96-00029-CV-1 (S.D. Ga. 1996)

FACTS

Haddle (plaintiff), a former at-will employee of Healthmaster Home Health Care, Inc., alleges that he was fired because he was planning to be a witness in a Federal criminal trial, and that the firing has caused him an actual injury. Haddle is suing his former employers for a violation of his civil rights under 42 U.S.C. § 1985(2), making it a crime to conspire to cause an injury to any witness in order to deter the witness from testifying in federal court.

I

Can employee state a valid cause of action by contending that his firing is an "injury" even if he was an at-will employee?

R

An at-will employee who was fired is not "injured," such that a claim for injury cannot be sustained, as a matter of law.

A

Rule 12(b)(6) permits a defendant to move to dismiss a complaint on the ground that the complaint fails to state a claim upon which relief can be granted. In essence, the movant says, "Even if everything you allege is true, the law affords you no relief." In deciding a 12(b)(6) motion, a court must assume that all of the factual allegations in the complaint are true. Turning to the facts and issue of the instant case, we note that plaintiff Haddle claims that his allegations will sustain a cause of action under §1985(2) despite his status as an at-will employee. We disagree. Haddle's claim is contrary to binding 11th Circuit precedent in *Morast v. Lance,* which held that a plaintiff must have been actually injured in order to sustain a claim under § 1985(2), and the discharge of an at-will employee is not an actual injury. As a result, under *Morast,* Haddle has not been legally "injured," and has therefore not stated a claim upon which relief can be granted.

C

Dismissed.

Haddle v. Garrison (11th Cir. 1996)

Unpublished Opinion. Docket No. 96-8856 (11th Cir. 1996)

FACTS

Haddle (plaintiff), a former at-will employee of Healthmaster Home Health Care, Inc., alleges that he was fired because he was planning to be a witness in a Federal criminal trial, and that the firing has caused him an actual injury. Haddle is suing his former employers for a violation of his civil rights under 42 U.S.C. §1985(2), making it a crime to conspire to cause an injury to any witness in order to deter the witness from testifying in federal court. Plaintiff appeals from the judgment of the lower court.

I

Can employee state a valid cause of action by contending that his firing is an "injury" even if he was an at-will employee?

R

An at-will employee who was fired is not "injured," such that a claim for injury cannot be sustained, as a matter of law.

A

Rule 12(b)(6) permits a defendant to move to dismiss a complaint on the ground that the complaint fails to state a claim upon which relief can be granted. In essence, the movant says, "Even if everything you allege is true, the law affords you no relief." In deciding a 12(b)(6) motion, a court must assume that all of the factual allegations in the complaint are true. Turning to the facts and issue of the instant case, we note that plaintiff Haddle claims that his allegations will sustain a cause of action under §1985(2) despite his status as an at-will employee. We disagree. Haddle's claim is contrary to binding 11th Circuit precedent in *Morast v. Lance,* which held that a plaintiff must have been actually injured in order to sustain a claim under § 1985(2), and the discharge of an at-will employee is not an actual injury. As a result, under *Morast,* Haddle has not been legally "injured," and has therefore not stated a claim upon which relief can be granted.

C

Judgment of the lower court affirmed.

Haddle v. Garrison

U.S. Supreme Court, 525 U.S. 121 (1998)

FACTS

Petitioner, an at-will employee, sued for damages against respondents alleging that they conspired to have him fired in retaliation for obeying a federal grand jury subpoena and to deter him from testifying at their upcoming criminal trial for Medicare fraud, and that their acts had "injured [him] in his person or property" in violation of 42 U. S. C. §1985(2). In dismissing the suit for failure to state a claim, the District Court relied on Circuit precedent holding that an at-will employee discharged pursuant to a conspiracy proscribed by §1985(2) has suffered no actual injury because he has no constitutionally protected interest in continued employment. The 11th Circuit affirmed.

I

Must an at-will employee, discharged pursuant to a conspiracy proscribed by §1985(2), suffer an injury to a "constitutionally protected property interest" to state a claim?

R

A petitioner need not suffer an injury to a "constitutionally protected property interest" to state a claim under §1985.

A

The sort of the harm alleged by petitioner, essentially third-party interference with at-will employment relationships, states a claim for damages under §1985(2). In relevant part, the statute proscribes conspiracies to "deter, by force, intimidation, or threat, any ... witness in any [federal] court ... from attending such court, or from testifying in any matter pending therein, ... or to injure [him] in his person or property on account of his having so attended or testified," §1985(2), and provides that if conspirators "do ... any act in furtherance of ... such conspiracy, whereby another is injured in his person or property, . . . the party so injured ... may" recover damages, §1985(3). The 11th Circuit erred in concluding that petitioner must suffer an injury to a "constitutionally protected property interest" to state a claim. Nothing in the language or purpose of the proscriptions in the first clause of §1985(2), nor in its attendant remedial provisions, establishes such a requirement. The gist of the wrong at which §1985(2) is directed is not deprivation of property, but intimidation or retaliation against witnesses in federal-court proceedings. The terms "injured in his person or property" define the harm that the victim may suffer as a result of the conspiracy to intimidate or retaliate. Thus, the fact that employment at will is not "property" for purposes of the Due Process Clause does not mean that loss of at-will employment may not "injur[e] [petitioner] in his person or property" for §1985(2)'s purposes. Such harm has long been, and remains, a compensable injury under tort law.

C

Reversed and remanded.

Bell Atlantic Corp. v. Twombly

U.S. Supreme Court, 127 S.Ct. 1955 (2007)

BACKGROUND

The 1984 divestiture of AT&T's local telephone business left a system of regional service monopolies, sometimes called Incumbent Local Exchange Carriers (ILECs), and a separate long-distance market from which the ILECs were excluded. The Telecommunications Act of 1996 withdrew approval of the ILECs' monopolies, "fundamentally restructuring local telephone markets" and "subjecting ILECs to a host of duties intended to facilitate market entry." It also authorized them to enter the long-distance market. Central to the new scheme was each ILEC's obligation to share its network with competitive local exchange carriers (CLECs).

FACTS

Respondents (hereinafter plaintiffs) represent a class of subscribers of local telephone and/or high speed Internet services in this action against petitioner ILECs for claimed violations of §1 of the Sherman Act, which prohibits "[e]very contract, combination in the form of trust or otherwise, or conspiracy, in restraint of trade or commerce among the several States, or with foreign nations." The complaint alleges that the ILECs conspired to restrain trade (1) by engaging in parallel conduct in their respective service areas to inhibit the growth of upstart CLECs; and (2) by agreeing to refrain from competing against one another, as indicated by their common failure to pursue attractive business opportunities in contiguous markets and by a statement by one ILEC's chief executive officer that competing in another ILEC's territory did not seem right. The District Court dismissed the complaint, concluding that parallel business conduct allegations, taken alone, do not state a claim under §1; plaintiffs must allege additional facts tending to exclude independent self-interested conduct as an explanation for the parallel actions. Reversing, the Second Circuit held that plaintiffs' parallel conduct allegations were sufficient to withstand a motion to dismiss because the ILECs failed to show that there is no set of facts that would permit plaintiffs to demonstrate that the particular parallelism asserted was the product of collusion rather than coincidence.

I

Did respondents adequately state their complaint with enough factual matter (taken as true) to suggest that an agreement was made?

R

Stating a §1 claim requires a complaint with enough factual matter (taken as true) to suggest that an agreement was made. An allegation of parallel conduct and a bare assertion of conspiracy will not suffice.

A

Because §1 prohibits "only restraints effected by a contract, combination, or conspiracy," the crucial question is whether the challenged anticompetitive conduct "stem[s] from independent decision or from an

---

agreement." While a showing of parallel "business behavior is admissible circumstantial evidence from which" agreement may be inferred, it falls short of "conclusively establish[ing] agreement or ... itself constitut[ing] a Sherman Act offense." The inadequacy of showing parallel conduct or interdependence, without more, mirrors the behavior's ambiguity: consistent with conspiracy, but just as much in line with a wide swath of rational and competitive business strategy unilaterally prompted by common perceptions of the market. Thus, this Court has hedged against false inferences from identical behavior at a number of points in the trial sequence, *e.g.,* at the summary judgment stage.

This case presents the antecedent question of what a plaintiff must plead in order to state a §1 claim. Federal Rule of Civil Procedure 8(a)(2) requires only "a short and plain statement of the claim showing that the pleader is entitled to relief," in order to "give the defendant fair notice of what the ... claim is and the grounds upon which it rests," *Conley* v. *Gibson*, 355 U. S. 41 . While a complaint attacked by a Rule 12(b)(6) motion to dismiss does not need detailed factual allegations, *ibid.,* a plaintiff's obligation to provide the "grounds" of his "entitle[ment] to relief" requires more than labels and conclusions, and a formulaic recitation of a cause of action's elements will not do. Factual allegations must be enough to raise a right to relief above the speculative level on the assumption that all of the complaint's allegations are true. Applying these general standards to a §1 claim, stating a claim requires a complaint with enough factual matter to suggest an agreement.

Under the plausibility standard, plaintiffs' claim of conspiracy in restraint of trade comes up short. First, the complaint leaves no doubt that plaintiffs rest their §1 claim on descriptions of parallel conduct, not on any independent allegation of actual agreement among the ILECs. The nub of the complaint is the ILECs' parallel behavior, and its sufficiency turns on the suggestions raised by this conduct when viewed in light of common economic experience. Nothing in the complaint invests either the action or inaction alleged with a plausible conspiracy suggestion. As to the ILECs' supposed agreement to disobey the 1996 Act and thwart the CLECs' attempts to compete, the District Court correctly found that nothing in the complaint intimates that resisting the upstarts was anything more than the natural, unilateral reaction of each ILEC intent on preserving its regional dominance. The complaint's general collusion premise fails to answer the point that there was no need for joint encouragement to resist the 1996 Act, since each ILEC had reason to try and avoid dealing with CLECs and would have tried to keep them out, regardless of the other ILECs' actions. Plaintiffs' second conspiracy theory rests on the competitive reticence among the ILECs themselves in the wake of the 1996 Act to enter into their competitors' territories, leaving the relevant market highly compartmentalized geographically, with minimal competition. This parallel conduct did not suggest conspiracy, not if history teaches anything. Monopoly was the norm in telecommunications, not the exception. Because the ILECs were born in that world, doubtless liked it, and surely knew the adage about him who lives by the sword, a natural explanation for the noncompetition is that the former Government-sanctioned monopolists were sitting tight, expecting their neighbors to do the same. Antitrust conspiracy was not suggested by the facts adduced under either theory of the complaint, which thus fails to state a valid §1 claim. Here, the Court is not requiring heightened fact pleading of specifics, but only enough facts to state a claim to relief that is plausible on its face. Because the plaintiffs here have not nudged their claims across the line from conceivable to plausible, their complaint must be dismissed.

C

Reversed and Remanded.

Stradford v. Zurich Insurance Co.

2002 WL 31027517 (S.D.N.Y. 2002)

FACTS

On August 18, 1999, plaintiff Stradford, a dentist with an office in New York, took out an insurance policy on his office from defendant Northern, an insurance company affiliated with the Zurich Insurance Co. (defendant). Northern cancelled the policy from October 10, 1999 to December 13, 1999, because Dr. Stradford failed to pay his premiums. After Stradford delivered a "no claims" letter indicating that he had no losses during the period of interruption, Northern reinstated the policy on December 14, 1999 and notified Stradford of the reinstatement on January 9, 2000. Less than 10 days later, on January 17, 2000, Stradford filed a claim under the policy seeking coverage of $151,154.74 in damage to his personal property and inventory as a result of a water leak. After Northern paid the claim, Stradford submitted an amended claim seeking $1,385,456.70 for damage to personal property and business interruption. Northern investigated the claim and concluded that the loss occurred during the period that the policy had lapsed, and it therefore denied the claim. Consequently, Stradford sued Northern in federal district court, and Northern counterclaimed for the return of the money paid on the initial claim and punitive damages for Stradford's willful attempts to defraud the defendants. Stradford moved to dismiss the counterclaim under Rule 9(b); that is, for a failure to state claims of fraud with particularity.

I Do general statements of fraud satisfy Rule 9(b)?

R Claims of fraud or mistake under Rule 9(b) must be asserted with particularity to provide the opposing party fair notice of the claim and the grounds on which it is based; particularity requires an affirmative allegation of the time, place, and manner in which the fraud occurred.

A Rule 9(b) requires all allegations of fraud or mistake to be asserted with particularity, while malice, intent, knowledge, and other states of mind may be asserted generally. In this case, the counterclaim asserts general facts which allow the inference that Stradford intended to defraud Northern, but fails to set forth the allegations of fraud with any particularity. Particularity requires an affirmative allegation of the time, place, and manner in which the fraud occurred. This the counterclaim failed to do. Without such a showing, the counterclaim fails to provide Stradford fair notice of the claims against him as required by the Rules. However, leave to amend should be granted to provide a party the opportunity to assert its claims with particularity when a defendant has not previously had an opportunity to do so.

C Motion denied with leave to amend.

Jones v. Block

U.S. Supreme Court, 127 S.Ct. 910 (2007)

FACTS

The Prison Litigation Reform Act of 1995 (PLRA), in order to address the large number of prisoner complaints filed in federal court, mandates early judicial screening of prisoner complaints and requires prisoners to exhaust prison grievance procedures before filing suit. 42 U. S. C. §1997e(a). Petitioners, inmates in Michigan prisons, filed grievances using the Michigan Department of Corrections (MDOC) grievance process. After unsuccessfully seeking redress through that process, petitioner Jones filed a 42 U. S. C. §1983 suit against six prison officials. The District Court dismissed on the merits as to four of them and as to two others found that Jones had failed to adequately plead exhaustion in his complaint. Petitioner Williams also filed a §1983 suit after his two MDOC grievances were denied. The District Court found that he had not exhausted his administrative remedies with regard to one of the grievances because he had not identified any of the respondents named in the lawsuit during the grievance process. While the court found Williams's other claim properly exhausted, it dismissed the entire suit under the Sixth Circuit's total exhaustion rule for PLRA cases. Petitioner Walton's §1983 lawsuit also was dismissed under the total exhaustion rule because his MDOC grievance named only one of the six defendants in his lawsuit. The Sixth Circuit affirmed in each case, relying on its procedural rules that require a prisoner to allege and demonstrate exhaustion in his complaint, permit suit only against defendants identified in the prisoner's grievance, and require courts to dismiss the entire action if the prisoner fails to satisfy the exhaustion requirement as to any single claim in his complaint.

I

Are the Sixth Circuit's rules are required by the PLRA?

R

The Sixth Circuit's rules are not required by the PLRA, and crafting and imposing such rules exceeds the proper limits of the judicial role.

A

Failure to exhaust is an affirmative defense under the PLRA, and inmates are not required to specially plead or demonstrate exhaustion in their complaints. There is no question that exhaustion is mandatory under the PLRA, but it is less clear whether the prisoner must plead and demonstrate exhaustion in the complaint or the defendant must raise lack of exhaustion as an affirmative defense. Failure to exhaust is better viewed as an affirmative defense. Federal Rule of Civil Procedure 8(a) requires simply a "short and plain statement of the claim" in a complaint, and PLRA claims are typically brought under 42 U. S. C. §1983, which does not require exhaustion at all. The fact that the PLRA dealt extensively with exhaustion, but is silent on the issue whether exhaustion must be pleaded or is an affirmative defense, is strong evidence that the usual practice should be followed, and the practice under the Federal Rules is to regard exhaustion as an affirmative defense, including in the similar statutory scheme governing habeas corpus. Courts should generally not depart from the Federal Rules' usual practice based on perceived policy concerns.

Exhaustion is not *per se* inadequate under the PLRA when an individual later sued was not named in the grievance. Nothing in the MDOC policy supports the conclusion that the grievance process was improperly invoked because an individual later named as a defendant was not named at the first step of the process; at the time each grievance was filed here, the MDOC policy did not specifically require a prisoner to name anyone in the grievance. Nor does the PLRA impose such a requirement. The "applicable procedural rules" that a prisoner must properly exhaust are defined not by the PLRA, but by the prison grievance process itself. As the MDOC's procedures make no mention of naming particular officials, the Sixth Circuit's rule imposing such a prerequisite to proper exhaustion is unwarranted. The Circuit's rule may promote early notice to those who might later be sued, but that has not been thought to be one of the leading purposes of the exhaustion requirement. The court below should determine in the first instance whether petitioners' grievances otherwise satisfied the exhaustion requirement.

The PLRA does not require dismissal of the entire complaint when a prisoner has failed to exhaust some, but not all, of the claims included in the complaint. Respondents argue that had Congress intended courts to dismiss only unexhausted claims while retaining the balance of the lawsuit, it would have used the word "claim" instead of "action" in §1997e(a), which provides that "[n]o action shall be brought" unless administrative procedures are exhausted. That boilerplate language is used in many instances in the Federal Code, and statutory references to an "action" have not typically been read to mean that every claim included in the action must meet the pertinent requirement before the "action" may proceed. If a complaint contains both good and bad claims, the court proceeds with the good and leaves the bad. Respondents note that the total exhaustion requirement in habeas corpus is an exception to this general rule, but a court presented with a mixed habeas petition typically "allow[s] the petitioner to delete the unexhausted claims and to proceed with the exhausted claims, which is the opposite of the rule the Sixth Circuit adopted, and precisely the rule that respondents argue against. Although other PLRA sections distinguish between actions and claims, respondents' reading of §1997e(a) creates its own inconsistencies, and their policy arguments are also unpersuasive.

C No. 05-7058, 135 Fed. Appx. 837; No. 05-7142, 136 Fed. Appx. 846 (second judgment) and 859 (first judgment), reversed and remanded.

Walker v. Northwest Corp.

108 F.3d 158 (8th Cir. 1996)

FACTS

Plaintiff-minor Jimmy Lee Walker III, his guardian, Cynthia Walker, and their attorney James Harrison Massey, filed a complaint against Norwest Corp. (defendant) and others in federal district court concerning a dispute over his trust fund. In the complaint, Massey alleged diversity jurisdiction and stated that "the Plaintiff and ***some*** of the Defendants are citizens of different states." Specifically, the complaint alleged that all plaintiffs were South Dakota citizens and that Norwest Corp. was a Minnesota corporation, but failed to allege the citizenship of the remaining defendants. Norwest filed a motion to dismiss and a request for sanctions after alerting Massey that the complaint failed to properly allege diversity jurisdiction and requesting his voluntary dismissal of the complaint, which was not done. The federal district court granted the motion to dismiss and ordered Massey to pay $4,800 in attorneys' fees and costs as a sanction.

I

Should a court impose monetary sanctions on the moving party's attorney when that attorney fails to assert the diversity of citizenship of ***all*** defendants in a complaint in an appropriate action asserting diversity jurisdiction?

R

Sanctions are appropriate when an attorney raises allegations or factual contentions that are not supported by evidence or likely to be supported upon reasonable discovery.

A

Under Rule 11, a court may impose sanctions upon an attorney if it determines that the allegations and factual contentions raised in any pleading, motion, or court submission are not supported by evidence or, with a reasonable opportunity to investigate, are not likely to be supported by evidence. In the instant case, plaintiffs contend that Rule 11 does not require the level of "in-depth and possibly impossible" investigation required to determine the true citizenship of each defendant before filing their complaint. We disagree. It is the plaintiffs' burden to plead the citizenship of each defendant when asserting diversity jurisdiction. Thus, at a minimum, plaintiffs must allege in their complaint that none of the defendants share a common citizenship with the plaintiffs. Because they failed to do so, the court did not abuse its discretion by imposing sanctions. Monetary sanctions were appropriate.

C

Affirmed

Christian v. Mattell Inc.

222286 F.3d 1118 (9th Cir. 2003)

FACTS

Claudene Christian (plaintiff), then an undergraduate at USC, created and marketed a college doll that resembled a USC cheerleader with blond hair and blue eyes. She held a valid copyright to her creation. Six years later, Mattel, Inc. (defendant) created a similar-looking Barbie doll. Mattel had been producing the Barbie doll since 1959, which has evolved over the decades. Christian, through her attorney James Hicks, sued Mattel in federal district court for copyright infringement, seeking $2.4 million in damages and injunctive relief. Two months later, Mattel moved for summary judgment, demonstrating that it had obtained the copyright for the sculpture of its doll's head years before Christian obtained her copyright. In a follow-up meeting between Hicks and Mattel's attorneys required by a local rule, Mattel attempted to persuade Hicks to dismiss the complaint as frivolous. Hicks refused and Mattel thereafter motioned for Rule 11 sanctions, which was granted by the court. The court found that Hicks had filed a meritless complaint without any factual foundation and further found Hicks guilty of attorney misconduct. Hicks was ordered to pay Mattel $501,565 in attorneys' fees.

I Did the court abuse its discretion by imposing sanctions on plaintiff's attorney?

R Under Rule 11, a court may impose sanctions upon an attorney if it determines that the allegations and factual contentions in any pleading, motion, or other court submission are not supported by evidence or, with a reasonable opportunity to investigate, are not likely to be supported by evidence.

A Under Rule 11, a court may impose sanctions upon an attorney if it determines that the allegations and factual contentions in any pleading, motion, or other court submission are not supported by evidence or, with a reasonable opportunity to investigate, are not likely to be supported by evidence. The rule is, however, limited to court documents signed by an attorney and a court may not impose Rule 11 sanctions for misconduct not involving signed court submissions. Here, we hold that court did not abuse its discretion in imposing sanctions related to Hicks's failure to investigate the status of Mattel's copyright, but it did err in considering other instances of misconduct. A court may impose sanctions against those appearing in the courtroom ***only*** upon "an explicit finding that counsel's conduct constituted or was tantamount to bad faith." This the lower court failed to do. As a consequence, the court abused its discretion by imposing sanctions on the totality of Hicks's conduct.

C Remanded.

Zielinski v. Philadelphia Piers Inc.

U.S. District Court, 139 F.Supp. 408 (E.D. Pa. 1956)

FACTS

When his forklift was struck by another forklift, the plaintiff suffered injuries and initiated this lawsuit. Plaintiff Zielinski sued Defendant Philadelphia Piers Inc. (PPI) because the forklift which collided with his had "PPI" written on its side. Plaintiff assumed there was an agency relationship between the driver of the other forklift, Johnson, and Defendant PPI, his "employer" at the time. After the complaint was served, Defendant PPI answered and referred to itself as "defendant" within the answer. Afterwards, the complaint was forwarded to PPI's insurance company which acknowledged responsibility as well. However, at trial, information came to light that the defendant had sold its freight moving unit to Carload Contractors and that Johnson was switched over to Carload's payroll. Thus, Defendant PPI no longer believed it should be held accountable for Plaintiff Zielinski's injuries and generally denied the allegations in the plaintiff's complaint. Zielinski responded by filing a motion for a ruling on the issue of an agency relationship between Johnson and the defendant and that Zielinski was in fact suing the right defendant.

I

When at least some of the allegations being denied have been admitted by both parties as true, is a general denial valid?

R

If ANY of the allegations being denied have been admitted as true by both parties, a general denial will NOT be valid.

A

A general denial will not be valid if any of the allegations being denied have previously been admitted as true by both parties. In such a circumstance, the defendant must make a more specific answer. In the instant case, when Plaintiff Zielinski stated in his pleadings that he was injured by another forklift operated by Defendant PPI, a general denial by PPI is plainly erroneous. It implies not only the denial that the forklift was operated by an agent of the Defendant PPI, but also that he (Plaintiff Zielinski) was not injured; which cannot be denied because it was previously admitted as a true fact. Two policy considerations support our finding: (1) Defendant PPI knows that the statute of limitations has run. Therefore, dismissing the complaint would effectively deprive the plaintiff of any opportunity to redress; and (2) when an improper and ineffective answer has been filed knowingly after the plaintiff's statute of limitations has run, an allegation of agency will be instructed to the jury as presumptively admitted by both parties for the purpose of the litigation.

C

No. If any of the allegations being denied have been admitted as true by both parties, a general denial will not be valid.

Beeck v. Aquaslide 'N' Dive Corp.

U.S. Court of Appeals, 562 F.2d 537 (8th Cir. 1977)

FACTS

Beeck (plaintiff) was severely injured while using a water slide he claims was negligently manufactured by Aquaslide (defendant) located in the Village of Kimberly. The Village investigated the matter and stated that the slide was manufactured by Aquaslide. Plaintiff Beeck filed his personal injury complaint against Aquaslide, which the defendant answered admitting that it "designed, manufactured, assembled and sold" the slide. About 6 months after the statute of limitations had run out and a total of about one year after filing the complaint and answer, the President of Aquaslide visited the site and determined that the slide was not an Aquaslide product. The defendant thereafter moved to amend its answer to deny the slide's manufacture. The court granted the motion and Plaintiff Beeck appealed. The court then granted a separate trial to decide the issue of manufacture which plaintiff lost and then appealed.

I

May a trial court allow the defendant's answer to be amended from an initial admission to a denial as it relates to a party's responsibility for the manufacture of the product at issue?

R

A trial court has discretion to allow an amendment to an answer from admitting or denying responsibility for the manufacture of the product at issue.

A

A trial court has discretion to allow an amendment to an answer from admitting or denying responsibility for the manufacture of the product at issue. In *Forman v. Davis* the Supreme Court held that, in the absence of bad faith on the part of the movant, leave to amend is fully in the discretion of the District Court. This holding is rooted in Rule 15(a), which provides that leave to amend should be "freely given where justice so requires." In the instant case, the trial court did not abuse its discretion by allowing the amendment as there was no evidence of bad faith. Moreover, as to plaintiff's contention of prejudice because the statute of limitations had run prior to the motion to amend, this presupposes that the trial court should have known the plaintiff would have lost on that issue at trial. That expectation is an unreasonable one.

C

Yes. A trial court has discretion to allow an amendment to an answer from admitting or denying responsibility for the manufacture of the product at issue.

Moore v. Baker

989 F.2d 1129 (11th Cir. 1993)

FACTS

Dr. Baker (defendant) performed surgery on Judith Moore (plaintiff) to remove a blockage of her carotid artery. Baker warned Moore about the surgery and its risks, and Moore signed a consent form. The operation went badly and Moore was permanently and severely disabled. Moore filed her complaint on the last day permitted by the state's statute of limitations, alleging that Baker had violated the state's informed consent law by failing to advise Moore of alternative therapy. She later moved to amend her complaint to include allegations of negligence against Baker. The district court denied the motion.

I

Will an amendment to a complaint relate back to the date of filing the original complaint?

R

A proposed amendment must have its basis in the same facts that are alleged in the original complaint in order for it to relate back to the time of the original complaint.

A

The statute of limitations will bar plaintiff's claim of negligence asserted in her amended complaint unless the amended complaint relates back to the time of the original complaint, which was filed just before the statute of limitations was about to run. Rule 15(c) permits an amended pleading to relate back to the date of the original pleading "whenever the claim or defense asserted in the amended pleading arose out of the conduct, transaction, or occurrence set forth or attempted to be set forth in the original pleading." The critical issue in Rule 15(c) is whether the original complaint gave notice to the defendant of the claim that is now being asserted. We find that it does not. The original complaint focused on defendant's actions before the surgery, whereas the amendment seeks to focus on his actions during and after the surgery. The alleged acts of negligence occurred at different times and involved separate and distinct conduct. Notice to Baker that Moore might claim that he was negligent is clearly lacking. In order to recover on her negligence claim, Moore would have to prove completely different facts than would otherwise have been required for the informed consent claim of the original complaint. We thus conclude that Moore's negligence claim does not arise out of the same conduct, transaction, or occurrence as the claims in the original complaint and, therefore, the proposed new claims are barred by the statute of limitations.

C

Affirmed.

Bonerb v. Richard J. Caron Foundation

156 F.R.D. 16 (W.D.N.Y. 1994)

FACTS

Plaintiff Bonerb sued Richard J. Caron Foundation's (defendant) drug and alcohol rehabilitation facility after he was injured following a slip-and-fall accident. Plaintiff was a patient at the facility and was injured while playing basketball as part of the Foundation's mandatory exercise program. Bonerb (plaintiff) initially claimed that the Foundation negligently maintained that basketball court, but later, one year after the complaint was filed and after the statute of limitations had run, filed a motion to amend his complaint to include a cause of action for counseling malpractice. The Foundation objected, claiming amendment is barred by the statute of limitations because the counseling malpractice claim does not relate back to the original pleading.

I

Does the malpractice claim relate back to the original negligence claim?

R

A claim will relate back if the operational facts set out in the original complaint are sufficient to put the defendant on notice that the amended claim could be brought.

A

Rule 15(a) provides that leave to amend a complaint should be freely granted absent undue prejudice to the other party, undue delay by the moving party, or bad faith. If the litigant has been advised at the outset of the general facts from which the late asserted claim arises, the amendment will relate back even though the statute of limitations may have run in the interim. A claim will relate back if the operational facts set out in the original complaint are sufficient to put the defendant on notice that the amended claim could be brought. The theory behind this rule is that one who has been given notice of litigation concerning a given transaction or occurrence has been provided with all the protection that statutes of limitation are designed to afford. Here, the allegations in the original and amended complaints derive from the same operative facts involving the injury suffered by plaintiff - the participation in the exercise program was mandatory and that plaintiff's injury was caused by the defendant's failure to properly supervise and instruct plaintiff. These allegations are sufficient to alert the defendant to the possibility of a related claim based on negligent performance.

C

Motion granted.

Davis v. Precoat Metals

2002 WL 1759828 (N.D. Ill. 2002)

FACTS

Several plaintiffs, including Nicholas sued defendant Precoat Metals under Title VII of the Civil Rights Act of 1964 alleging discrimination on the basis of race and national origin. Plaintiffs alleged that while employed by defendant, they were subjected to racial comments by management-level employees; suffered discrimination in their job placement, work assignments, promotions and discipline; and suffered retaliation after reporting the alleged acts of discrimination. During discovery, the plaintiffs requested that the defendant disclose any past racial or national origin discrimination complaints asserted against it by its past/present employees. The defendants refused, arguing that the request was overbroad and that such complaints were not relevant to the instant case/claims. Plaintiffs motioned the court to compel discovery under Rule 26(b)(1).

I

Are complaints relating to past race and national origin discrimination against the defendants relevant to the plaintiffs' discovery requests regarding their present claims?

R

A party may seek discovery of any past or present matter which is not privileged and which is relevant to the claim or defense of any party providing the request cannot be obtained from a source which is more convenient, less burdensome or less expensive or the burden of the expense of the proposed discovery does not outweigh its likely benefit.

A

Under Rule 26(b)(1), a party may seek discovery of "any matter, not privileged, that is relevant to the claim or defense of any party," and it need not be admissible at trial. Information is relevant when it is "reasonably calculated to lead to the discovery of admissible evidence" providing the request cannot be obtained from a source which is more convenient, less burdensome or less expensive or the burden of the expense of the proposed discovery does not outweigh its likely benefit. If it does, the court may preclude or limit discovery. In the instant case, the plaintiffs have limited their request to a specific period of time, limited their complaints to those affecting race and national origin discrimination, and confined their complaints to the specific plant in which they worked. The plaintiffs' request is relevant to their present claims and has been narrowly tailored to specific discoverable information. Accordingly, the defendants must disclose the information requested.

C

Motion granted.

Steffan v. Cheney

920 F.2d 74 (D.C. Cir. 1990)

FACTS

Plaintiff Joseph C. Steffan was a naval officer who resigned from the military in 1987 after an administrative board recommended his discharge. Specifically, plaintiff was discharged after he admitted that he was a homosexual, though he was not discharged for any conduct relating thereto. In 1988, Steffan filed an action against the U.S. Government (defendant), represented by then Secretary of Defense, Dick Cheney, to challenge the constitutionality of the regulations that required the discharge of admitted homosexuals. During discovery, plaintiff refused to answer deposition questions regarding whether he engaged in homosexual conduct during or after his tenure as a midshipman while in the Navy. He also raised and asserted his Fifth Amendment privilege against self-incrimination. The district court dismissed plaintiff's case for failure to comply with the discovery order and plaintiff thereafter appealed to the appellate court.

I

Is evidence considered relevant if it does not relate to a matter pertinent to a decision of the case?

R

Evidence is not considered relevant if it does not relate to a matter pertinent to a decision of the case.

A

The district court acknowledged that Steffan was separated from the naval academy based on his ***admission*** that he is a homosexual, and was not based on any evidence of homosexual ***conduct***. However, the lower court found that questions about his homosexual conduct were "highly relevant" to the case because the navy could discharge individuals based on homosexual acts. However, in *SEC v. Chenery Corp.*, the U.S. Supreme Court held that any judicial review of an administrative action, including administrative actions by the military, is confined to "the grounds upon which the record discloses that [the] action was based." Here, plaintiff is challenging the Navy's administrative action only in so far as it found him unfit for military service because he ***stated*** he was a homosexual. This was the basis for his discharge, so the issue of whether he engaged in potentially disqualifying conduct is irrelevant because it does not relate to a matter pertinent to the decision of the case. Therefore, the district court erred in finding that the issue of homosexual ***conduct*** was relevant, and, as such, its judgment is reversed and remanded for further proceedings consistent with this opinion.

C

See above.

Silvestri v. General Motors Corp.

271 F.3d 583 (4th Cir. 2001)

FACTS

Plaintiff Mark Silvestri sued defendant General Motors Corp. after the airbag in the Monte Carlo he was driving failed to deploy when he hit a utility pole, causing him injuries. While he was in the hospital, his parents retained an attorney, who retained two accident reconstruction experts to examine the vehicle. They concluded that the airbag was defective, and told Silvestri's attorney that he should let General Motors see the vehicle. Neither Silvestri nor his lawyer took steps to preserve the vehicle or to notify General Motors of the existence of the vehicle, until almost three years later when Silvestri began this action. The district court dismissed the case for the spoliation of evidence.

I

Does a party's duty to preserve material evidence extend to the period before litigation, when a party reasonably should know that the evidence may be relevant to anticipated litigation, and therefore the object of discovery?

R

A party's duty to preserve material evidence extends to the period before litigation, when a party reasonably should know that the evidence may be relevant to anticipated litigation, and therefore the object of discovery.

A

Yes. A party's duty to preserve material evidence extends to the period before litigation, when a party reasonably should know that the evidence may be relevant to anticipated litigation, and therefore the object of discovery. Silvestri had access to the vehicle, and the vehicle was preserved in its post-accident condition for two to three months, or more, during which time Silvestri or his lawyer and his experts recognized not only that they would be suing General Motors but also that General Motors should be given the opportunity to inspect the vehicle. Silvestri therefore breached his duty not to spoliate evidence. And while dismissal is severe and constitutes the ultimate sanction for spoliation, it is necessary here because the prejudice to General Motors is extraordinary, denying it the ability to adequately defend its case..

C

Affirmed.

Hickman v. Taylor

U.S. Supreme Court, 329 U.S. 495 (1947)

FACTS

After the sinking of the tugboat, the J.M. Taylor, an accident which killed five crew members, Plaintiff Hickman, the representative of a deceased crew member, brought suit against the tug owners and the Baltimore and Ohio Railroad, whose railroad cars were being tugged at the same time of the accident. The tug owners were represented by Fortenbaugh, an attorney who privately interviewed the survivors and other witnesses prior to the commencement of the lawsuit. Plaintiff Hickman submitted interrogatories to the top owners seeking the production of written statements and other items acquired by Fortenbaugh as well as detailed accounts of any oral statements made to Fortenbaugh. The tug owners through Fortenbaugh declined to answer some interrogatories or produce the documents and claimed that the request called for privileged matter and constituted an attempt to obtain Fortenbaugh's private files. The District Court held that the requested matter was not privileged and ordered the tug owners and Fortenbaugh to answer the interrogatories and produce the documents.

I Are an opposing attorney's notes acquired through interviews and witness testimony open to discovery?

C A party is not entitled to obtain copies of an opposing attorney's notes and items acquired from interviews with witnesses, without a showing of good cause.

A Not all of an attorney's files are open to discovery by the opposing party. Rule 26(b) provides limitations on discovery when the inquiry infringes upon recognized areas of privilege. In the instant case, the memoranda, statements and mental impressions at issue and in Fortenbaugh's possession fall outside of the scope of the attorney-client privilege. Nevertheless, they are not freely discoverable by the plaintiff. Plaintiff Hickman had adequate opportunity to seek discovery of the same basic facts through inquiries and production requests on Fortenbaugh and on the parties to the lawsuit and through direct interviews with witnesses themselves. Plaintiff Hickman showed no compelling reason why he should be entitled to the information in Fortenbaugh's files, and he did not indicate that the denial of such production would unduly prejudice the preparation of his case.

C No. A party is not entitled to obtain copies of an opposing attorney's notes and items acquired from interviews with witnesses, without a showing of good cause. Affirmed.

Thompson v. The Haskell Co.

65 F. Empl. Prac. Cas. (BNA) 1088 (M.D. Fla. 1994)

FACTS

Plaintiff Thompson sued her employer, defendant Haskell Company, and her supervisor, defendant Zona, for sexual harassment. Thompson alleged she was fired on June 5, 1992 because she did not give in to her supervisor's advances and that her firing left her emotionally injured. Defendant Thompson hired an attorney who retained a psychologist, Dr. Lucas, to perform a diagnostic review and personality profile of Thompson. On June 15, 1992, Dr. Lucas prepared a psychological report for plaintiff's prior counsel. Defendant Haskell Company sought discovery of Dr. Lucas' report and on May 13, 1994, plaintiff filed a motion for a protective order to prevent it from discovering the report. In support of her motion, plaintiff argued that Rules 26 (b)(3)-(4) protected the psychological report from discovery; and that Rule 26 (b)(4)(B) provides that opinions and facts held by a non-testifying expert who has been retained or employed by the opposing party in anticipation of litigation cannot be discovered except as provided for under Rule 35(b) or if there is a showing of exceptional circumstances.

I

Can a party compel discovery of the opinions or findings of a non-testifying expert's report, retained by the opposing party in preparation of litigation, if such information is highly relevant to the case/claims?

R

A party cannot compel discovery of the opinions or findings of a non-testifying expert hired by the opposing party in preparation of litigation ***unless*** there are no other practical means to obtain the facts and opinions contained in that report.

A

Dr. Lucas' psychological report is "highly probative" of plaintiff's depressed emotional state and was made just over a week after her termination. The report is discoverable under Rule 26 (b)(4) because the information contained therein cannot be obtained by other means. Under Rule 26 (b)(4), an opposing party's expert's opinions or facts retained in anticipation of litigation ***cannot*** be discovered ***unless*** exceptional circumstances make it impracticable for the party to discover the facts or opinions by other means. Here, there exists no other report which assessed the plaintiff's state of mind made during the weeks immediately following her termination. Therefore, exceptional circumstances exist which allow for the disclosure of psychological report.

C

Motion is denied.

Chiquita International Ltd. v. M/V Bolero Reefer

1994 U.S. Dist. LEXIS 5820 (S.D.N.Y. 1994)

FACTS

Plaintiff Chiquita International employed defendant International Reefer Services S.A. to ship 154,660 boxes of bananas from Ecuador to Germany aboard the ship *Bolero Reefer*. However, because of alleged malfunctions in the ship's loading cranes only 111,660 boxes were loaded. The remaining 43,000 boxes of bananas were left in Ecuador and discarded. Moreover, the incomplete shipment that did arrive in Germany arrived in poor condition. Shortly after the ship arrived in Germany, Chiquita International hired Joseph Winer, a marine surveyor, to examine the ship and the loading gear. After the inspection, Chiquita International sued International Reefer. International Reefer sought to depose Mr. Winer as a witness and compel the disclosure of documents he prepared in connection with his inspection. Chiquita objected, arguing that Mr. Winer is a non-testifying expert who is protected from discovery under Rule 26 (b)(4)(B). On the other hand, International Reefer claims that Mr. Winer is not an expert but simply a witness, and, even if he were an expert, discovery should be allowed because he was the only examiner and the only person with knowledge of the condition of the vessel shortly after it arrived in Germany.

I Should discovery of an opposing party's non-testifying expert be permitted under the "exceptional circumstances" clause to Rule 26(b)(4)(B) even when the party seeking discovery had an opportunity to examine the subject of the expert's opinion?

R Discovery of an opposing party's non-testifying expert cannot be permitted under the exceptional circumstances exception where the party seeking discovery had an opportunity to examine the subject of the expert's opinion itself.

A A non-testifying expert is shielded from discovery if no exceptional circumstances exist which would make it impossible or highly impracticable for the party seeking the information to obtain facts or opinions on the same subject by other means. Here, Mr. Winer qualifies as a non-testifying expert because he is a marine engineer, who possesses a technical background and knowledge on the subject at issue, who was hired by the plaintiff to inspect the vessel and because the plaintiff is not calling him as a witness. Firsthand knowledge is not what qualifies him as an expert. The Federal Rules allow experts to base their opinions on their own firsthand investigations or on the information provided by others. Thus, distinguishing between fact and opinion is irrelevant and Rule 26(b)(4)(B) applies. International Reefer attempts to invoke the "exceptional circumstances" clause to Rule 26(b)(4)(B) arguing that discovery still should be permitted because exceptional circumstances existed. We disagree since International Reefer had an opportunity to send its own expert to the scene when the ship arrived in Germany, and nothing prevented such an inspection of the ship by it or its agents. Therefore, permitting discovery where International Reefer failed to hire, in a timely manner, its own marine surveyor to investigate "would permit the exceptional circumstances exception to swallow Rule 26 (b)(4)(B)." Nevertheless, International Reefer may discover information provided to Mr. Winer by others as long as this information does not reflect Mr. Winer's own observations or opinions. Therefore, plaintiff's request to take the deposition of Mr. Winer is denied and defendant Chiquita will produce only that information from Mr. Winer's files which ***do not*** contain his observations. Privileged information is similarly excluded.

C

See above.

Stalnaker v. Kmart Corp.

71 Fair Empl. Prac. Cas. (BNA) 705 (D. Kan. 1996)

FACTS

Plaintiff Stalnaker, a female employee of Kmart (defendant) corporation worked with Donald Graves (defendant) in the Receiving Department of Kmart. She filed suit against both defendants, Kmart and Graves, alleging that the latter created a hostile working environment and sexually harassed her by engaging in inappropriate touching. To that end, Stalnaker issued depositions for four non-party witnesses who had prior relationships with Graves. Graves opposed the motion and moved for a protective order protecting these witnesses from discovery, specifically with respect to any voluntary romantic conduct or any sexually related activities with him.

I

Can the discovery of information from a party or non-party be limited if it is potentially embarrassing and annoying?

R

A party seeking a protective order must establish "good cause" for the order and submit "a particular and specific demonstration of fact" whose effect it is to preclude inquiry into areas that are clearly outside the scope of appropriate discovery.

A

Rule 26 "permits a broad scope of discovery." A court may issue protective orders to either totally prohibit or limit the scope of discovery on certain matters. Rule 26(c) provides that a court has the discretion to issue a protective order upon good cause where "justice requires to protect a party or person from annoyance, embarrassment, oppression, or undue burden or expense" or where the inquiry reaches "into areas that are clearly outside the scope of appropriate discovery". The party seeking a protective order must establish good cause showing "a particular and specific demonstration of fact, as distinguished from stereotyped and conclusory statements." In addition, Rule 412 provides that "evidence offered to prove that any alleged victim has engaged in other sexual behavior" or "to prove the any alleged victim's sexual predisposition" is not admissible in criminal or civil actions involving sexual misconduct. The interplay between Rule 412 and Rules 26 and 26(c) is apparent. Rule 412 was designed to protect the victim of sexual abuse against invasion of privacy, embarrassment, and stereotyping that can be associated with the public disclosure of intimate sexual practices. However, the rule does not apply here because Graves is not the victim of a sexual act(s), she is the victim of sexual harassment. All the same, he has shown good cause to limit discovery of the non-party witnesses because (1) they have no relationship to the allegations against Kmart; (2) they were not involved in the creation of the hostile work environment, the sexual harassment claim, or otherwise wronged Stalnaker; (3) none of them complained about sexual harassment involving Graves; and (4) such activities will also constitute an invasion of their privacy. Plaintiff Stalnaker argues that these witnesses may possess relevant information about sexual harassment at Kmart. We agree. To that end, we limit discovery to an inquiry involving "any voluntary romantic or sexual activities with Mr.

Graves to the extent they show any conduct on his part to encourage, solicit, or influence any employee of Graves to engage or continue in such activities" and the parties will utilize any such discovery only for the purposes of litigation and the information will not be disclosed any third parties. We thus grant in part and overrule in part the defendant's motion for a protective order.

C

Granted in part and overruled in part the defendant's motion for a protective order.

Zubulake v. UBS Warburg LLP

220 F.R.D. 212 (S.D.N.Y. 2003)

FACTS

Plaintiff Laura Zubulake sued Defendant UBS Warburg LLC under federal, state and local laws for gender discrimination and illegal retaliation. She contends that key evidence is located in various emails exchanged among UBS employees that now exist only on Backup tapes and perhaps other archived media. According to defendant, restoring those emails would cost approximately $175,000, not including the cost of attorney billable time to reviewing them. Plaintiff now moves for an order compelling UBS to produce the emails at its expense.

I

Can the non-moving party be compelled to produce [and pay for] discovery in the form of electronically stored media, not easily accessible and produced at its own expense even if costly to produce?

R

A party is entitled to discovery of any document so long as it is relevant to its claims and the responding party bares the cost of producing the responsive media; however, when such information is not easily accessible and costly to produce, the court should consider a cost-shifting analysis.

A

Deciding disputes regarding the scope of discovery of electronic data requires a three-step analysis: 1) It is necessary for a court to thoroughly understanding the responding party's computer system both with respect to active and stored data. A court should consider cost-shifting only when electronic data is relatively inaccessible, such as in tape backups. 2) Because the cost-shifting is so fact-intensive, it is necessary to determine what data may be found on the inaccessible media. Requiring the responding party to restore a small sample of the requested backup tapes is a sensible approach. 3) Finally, in conducting the cost-shifting analysis, seven factors should be considered: i) the extent to which the request is specifically tailored to discover relevant information; ii) the availability of such information from other sources; iii) the total cost of production, compared to the amount in controversy; iv) the total cost of production, compared to the resources available to each party; v) the relative ability of each party to control costs and its incentive to do so; vi) the importance of the issues at stake in the litigation; and vi) the relative benefits to the parties of obtaining the information. In light of the above, we order UBS to produce all responsive emails that exist on its optical disks or on its active servers at its own expense [relatively accessible media] as well as responsive emails from five backup tapes selected by Zubulake [relatively inaccessible media]. UBS should then prepare an affidavit detailing the results of the search, as well as the time and money spent. After reviewing the contents of the backup tapes and UBS's certification, the court will conduct the appropriate cost shifting-analysis.

C

See Rule above.

Peralta v. Heights Medical Center

U.S. Supreme Court, 485 U.S. 80 (1988)

FACTS

In 1982, a default judgment was entered against appellant in appellee medical center's Texas state-court suit to recover a sum allegedly due under appellant's guarantee of a hospital debt incurred by one of his employees. The judgment was recorded, a writ of attachment was issued, and appellant's real property was sold to satisfy the judgment. In 1984, appellant initiated a bill of review proceeding seeking, inter alia, to set aside the default judgment and void the sale, and alleging that, since the original service of process itself showed it was untimely made and, in fact, he had never been personally served, the judgment was void under Texas law. The court entered summary judgment for appellee on the ground that it must be shown in a bill of review proceeding that the complainant had a meritorious defense to the action in which the judgment was entered, which appellant conceded he did not have. In affirming, the State Court of Appeals rejected appellant's contention that the meritorious-defense requirement violated his due process rights under the 14th Amendment. The State Supreme Court denied appellant's application for a writ of error, noting "No Reversible Error."

I Does a judgment entered without notice or service violates the Due Process Clause?

R A judgment entered without notice or service violates the Due Process Clause.

A The holding below contravenes this Court's precedents, under which a judgment entered without notice or service violates the Due Process Clause. The argument that appellant suffered no harm from the default judgment since the same judgment would again be entered on retrial absent a meritorious defense is untenable because, had he had notice of the suit, appellant might have impleaded the employee whose debt had been guaranteed, worked out a settlement, paid the debt, or sold the property himself rather than suffer its sale at a constable's auction for allegedly much less than its true value. Nor is there any doubt that the entry of the judgment itself had substantial adverse consequences, since the judgment was entered on county records, became a lien on appellant's property which impaired his ability to mortgage or alienate the property, and was the basis for issuance of the writ of execution under which the property was promptly sold, again without notice. The contention that appellant has other remedies to escape the consequences of an invalid judgment and should be left to pursue those avenues will not be considered here, since there is no indication that it was raised below.

C Reversed.

Matsushita Electric Industrial Co. v. Epstein

U.S. Supreme Court, 516 U.S. 367 (1996)

FACTS

A tender offer resulting in petitioner Matsushita Electric Industrial Co.'s acquisition of MCA, Inc., a Delaware corporation precipitated two lawsuits on behalf of MCA's stockholders. While the first, a Delaware class action based purely on state-law claims, was pending, the second suit was filed in a California federal court, alleging that Matsushita's tender offer violated certain Securities Exchange Commission Rules promulgated under the Securities Exchange Act of 1934 (Exchange Act). Section 27 of that Act confers exclusive jurisdiction upon the federal courts in such suits. Matsushita prevailed in the federal case, and while that judgment was on appeal, the parties to the state action reached a settlement, agreeing, inter alia, that class members who did not opt out of the class would waive all claims in connection with the tender offer, including those asserted in the California federal action. The Chancery Court approved the agreement, and the Delaware Supreme Court affirmed. Respondents are members of both the state and federal classes who did not opt out of the settlement class. In the instant case, the Ninth Circuit found that the Delaware judgment was not a bar to further prosecution of the federal action under the Full Faith and Credit Act, 28 U.S.C. 1738, and fashioned a test limiting the preclusive force of a state court settlement judgment to those claims that could "have been extinguished by the issue preclusive effect of an adjudication of the state claims."

I

May a federal court withhold full faith and credit from a state court judgment simply because the settlement releases claims within the exclusive jurisdiction of the federal courts?

R

Federal courts must give full faith and credit to state court judgments that release claims within the exclusive jurisdiction of the federal courts because the subject-matter jurisdiction exception to full faith and credit is inapposite where the rendering court had subject-matter jurisdiction over the underlying suit and the defendants.

A

The Delaware settlement judgment is entitled to full faith and credit, notwithstanding the fact that it released claims within the exclusive jurisdiction of the federal courts. Section 1738 - which directs federal courts to treat a state-court judgment with the same respect that it would receive in the rendering State's courts - is generally applicable in cases in which the state court judgment incorporates a class-action settlement releasing claims solely within the federal courts' jurisdiction. The judgment of a state court in a class action is plainly the product of a "judicial proceeding" within the meaning of 1738, and the fact that the judgment might bar litigation of exclusively federal claims does not necessarily make 1738 inapplicable, *Marrese v. American Academy of Orthopaedic Surgeons. Marrese* provides the analytical framework for deciding whether the Delaware judgment precludes this exclusively federal action. A federal court must first determine whether the rendering State's law indicates that the claim would be barred from litigation in a court of that State; if so, the federal court must decide whether, as an exception to 1738, it should refuse to give preclusive effect to the state-court judgment. Delaware Supreme Court cases have provided rules regarding the preclusive force of class-action settlement agreements in subsequent state-court suits and have also spoken to the effect of such judgments in federal court, indicating that when the Chancery Court approves a global release of claims, its settlement judgment will preclude on-going or future federal court litigation of any released claims. Thus, it appears that a Delaware court would give this settlement judgment preclusive effect in a subsequent proceeding, notwithstanding the fact that respondents could not have pressed their Exchange Act claims in the Chancery Court. The release in the judgment specifically refers to this lawsuit, the State courts found the settlement fair and the class notice adequate, and respondents acknowledge that they did not opt out of the class. Because it appears that the judgment would be res judicata under Delaware law, this Court must proceed to the second step of the *Marrese* analysis and ask whether 27 of the Exchange Act partially repealed 1738. Any such modification must be implied, but this Court has seldom, if ever, held that a federal statute impliedly repealed 1738. There is no suggestion in 27 that Congress meant to contravene the common-law rules of preclusion or to repeal 1738's express statutory requirement. Nor does 27 evince any intent to prevent a state-court litigant from voluntarily releasing Exchange Act claims in judicially approved settlements. Assuming that 27 is intended to serve at least the general purposes of achieving greater uniformity of construction and more effective and expert application of the Exchange Act, a state court Page III threatens neither purpose when it upholds a settlement releasing Exchange Act claims. In addition, other provisions of the Exchange Act suggest that Congress did not intend to create an exception to 1738 for suits alleging violations of the Act, and precedent supports the conclusion that the concerns underlying the grant of exclusive jurisdiction in 27 are not undermined by state-court approval of settlements releasing Exchange Act claims. Even when exclusively federal claims are at stake, there is no universal right to litigate such claims in federal court. The subject-matter jurisdiction exception to full faith and credit, relied on by the Ninth Circuit in this case, is inapposite here, where the rendering court had subject-matter jurisdiction over the underlying suit and the defendants.

C Reversed and remanded.

Kalinauskas v. Wong

151 F.R.D. 363 (D. Nev. 1993)

FACTS

Plaintiff Ms. Lin T. Kalinauskas, a former employee of defendant Caesar's Palace, sued the casino for sexual discrimination in the instant case. As part of discovery, Kalinauskas sought to depose Donna Thomas, another former employee who had settled a past sexual discrimination suit with Caesar's. That settlement, which the court had sealed upon stipulation by the parties, provided that Thomas was not to discuss any aspect of her employment at Caesar's. Defendant sought a Protective Order to prevent Thomas' deposition but the District Court denied the motion.

I

Is a confidential settlement agreement which was sealed by the court and entered into by private litigants, discoverable by a party in a separate lawsuit seeking information contained therein?

R

Courts may modify protective orders or settlement agreements to allow for the discovery of facts otherwise held confidential under the agreement.

A

Courts may modify protective orders or settlement agreements to allow for the discovery of facts otherwise sealed under the agreement. A modification can only be denied where it prejudices substantial rights of the opposing party, or where the prejudice outweighs the benefits of the modification. This case presents a direct conflict between the policies behind the public and private interests. To allow full discovery of sealed agreements would discourage such settlements in the future. Conversely, prohibiting discovery would condone buying the silence of a witness and would lead to repetitive and wasteful discovery. Here, Caesar's has not demonstrated any potential injury or prejudice which could arise from allowing the deposition. Moreover, we reject Caesar's contention that Kalinauskas must intervene in the Thomas case and seek modification of the order as that would be wasteful since no live controversy exists. Similarly, we reject the argument that Kalinauskas must show a compelling need to obtain discovery, since this only applies to the specific terms of the settlement and not to the factual circumstances surrounding the case. Accordingly, we will allow the deposition of Ms. Thomas, but such deposition may not disclose the substantive terms of the agreement.

C

Motion granted in part and denied in part.

Ferguson v. Countrywide Credit Industries Inc.

298 F.3d 778 (9th Cir. 2002)

FACTS

Plaintiff Misty Ferguson sued defendant Countrywide Credit Industries Inc. and her supervisor for sexual harassment, retaliation, and hostile work environment. Countrywide moved to compel the matter to arbitration pursuant to an employment contract, which required Ferguson to arbitrate her claims. The district court refused to compel arbitration, holding that the arbitration agreement was unenforceable under the doctrine of unconscionability.

I Is an arbitration agreement unconscionable, and therefore unenforceable, where it is a prerequisite to employment, job applicants are not permitted to modify the terms of the agreement, and the terms are one-sided, favoring the employer?

R An arbitration agreement is unconscionable, and therefore unenforceable, where it is a prerequisite to employment, job applicants are not permitted to modify the terms of the agreement, and the terms are one-sided, favoring the employer.

A Yes. An arbitration agreement is unconscionable and thus unenforceable, where it is a prerequisite to employment, job applicants are not permitted to modify the terms of the agreement, and the terms are one-sided, favoring the employer. A contract is unenforceable under the doctrine of unconscionability where there is both procedural and substantive unconscionability. Procedural unconscionability exists here, because the bargaining power of each party is unequal: Ferguson (P) had to sign the agreement, and accept all of its terms, or not get the job applied for. Substantive unconscionability also exists here, because the terms of the agreement are one-sided: The agreement compels arbitration of Ferguson's (P) claims, but exempts from arbitration the claims of Countrywide (D). In addition, Countrywide's (D) agreement requires Ferguson (P) to pay filing fees for arbitration, which could exceed the costs of litigation. Finally, the agreement includes limitations on the number of subjects Ferguson (P) could raise during discovery. While the discovery provision in the arbitration agreement is not so one-sided that it alone could be called unconscionable, in the context of an arbitration agreement that overall favors Countrywide (D), it too is unconscionable.

C Affirmed.

Carter v. Countrywide Credit Industries Inc.

362 F.3d 294 (5th Cir. 2004)

FACTS

Defendant Countrywide Credit Industries Inc. sells and services consumer mortgages. Plaintiffs Loy Carter, Geoff Burkhart, Heather Young and Deborah Robinson are current and former employees who sued under the FLSA, alleging that they were denied overtime pay. Countrywide moved to compel arbitration pursuant to individual agreements signed by each employee as a condition of employment. The employees argued that the arbitration agreements are unenforceable because their right to a judicial forum for FLSA claims cannot be waived and the agreements are procedurally and substantively unconscionable. They also claimed that arbitration would interfere with their substantive FLSA rights to proceed collectively, to collect attorneys' fees, to select their forum, and to engage in appropriate discovery, and that the cost-sharing provision imposes excessive costs that would prevent them from being able to arbitrate their claims. The Texas federal district court rejected most of the employees' arguments, but found that the provision in the arbitration agreements requiring the employees to pay half the arbitration costs would impose prohibitive costs. The court eliminated that provision pursuant to a severability clause, ordered Countrywide to pay all the arbitration costs, and granted the motion to compel arbitration.

I Are arbitration agreements providing that FLSA claims must be arbitrated per se unenforceable on the grounds that the employees' right to a judicial forum for FLSA claims cannot be waived?

R Arbitration agreements providing that Fair Labor Standards Act (FLSA) claims must be arbitrated are not per se unenforceable on the grounds that the employees' right to a judicial forum for FLSA claims cannot be waived..

A No. Arbitration agreements providing that FLSA claims must be arbitrated are not per se unenforceable on the grounds that the employees' right to a judicial forum for FLSA claims cannot be waived. There is a strong presumption in favor of arbitration and a party seeking to invalidate an arbitration agreement bears the burden of establishing its invalidity. Courts must enforce a party's commitment to arbitrate federal statutory claims unless the party can show that Congress intended to preclude arbitration or other nonjudicial resolution of those claims. There is nothing in the FLSA's text or legislative history indicating that it precludes arbitration. In addition, the arbitration agreements at issue in this case do not deprive the employees (P) of certain substantive rights guaranteed by the FLSA. A forum selection clause in the arbitration agreements requires that the arbitration be held in the federal judicial district in which the employee (P) was employed by Countrywide (D), and there is no evidence that this provision would prevent any of the employees (P) from vindicating their FLSA rights. The employees' (P) argument that the cost-sharing provision made arbitration prohibitively expensive for them was moot. In October 2000, Countrywide (D) sent a memorandum to all employees stating that they would only have to pay a $125 filing fee for arbitration and that the company (D) would pay all the other arbitration costs. The company formally acknowledged that the new policy will apply to the employees (P) in this case. Finally, the employees (P) argued that the arbitration agreements are procedurally and substantively unconscionable. Under Texas law, an arbitration agreement is not procedurally unconscionable simply because the employer was in a superior bargaining position, and in this case the agreements were not substantively unconscionable.

C Affirmed.

Ferguson v. Writers Guild of America, West

277 Cal. Rptr. 450 (1991)

FACTS

Plaintiff-appellant Larry Ferguson, a screenwriter, was hired by Paramount Pictures Corp. to write a screenplay for the movie "Beverly Hills Cop II." The Writers Guild (defendant-appellee) awarded Ferguson partial screenplay credit, but gave the story-line credit to two others. The process for determining writing credits was governed by two documents: a 369-page agreement and the Writers Guild West's credits manual. When a credit arbitration is requested, each party to the proceeding is allowed to peremptorily disqualified a reasonable number of arbitrators from a list of 400 composed by a Writers Guild secretary. The remaining arbitrators are then provided with all written material used in the creation of the screenplay. In this case, the arbitrators chosen held no hearing, and they deliberated independently of one other. Within 24 hours after the arbitrators reached their decision, Ferguson requested the policy review board to determine whether the "proceedings" substantially deviated from the policy of the Writers Guild. The board was not empowered. The policy review board approved the credit determination, which is a final decision. Thereafter, plaintiff sued citing procedural defects in the process, and appeals the superior court' ruling denying his requests to (1) depose the writer awarded credit, and (2) compel the Writers Guild to reveal the name of the arbitrators.

I May a court review the procedural rules adopted in an arbitration proceeding?

R Courts are limited in their power to review the final decision of arbitration panels.

A A court may not review the procedural rules adopted in an arbitration proceeding because judicial review of arbitration proceedings is limited to the final decision of arbitration panel. Under the agreement establishing the arbitration process, disputes over writing credits for movies are nonjusticiable. We note that the procedures adopted in the challenged arbitration have been reviewed for correctness by the policy review board. Because of their expertise, we accord the policy review board considerable deference. Ferguson did not specify to the review board the errors argued before this court, so he did not preserve for judicial review the contentions he has made.

C Appellant's motion to dismiss is denied and the judgment below affirmed.

Celotex Corp. v. Catrett

U.S. Supreme Court, 477 U.S. 317 (1986)

FACTS

The plaintiff sued the defendant for numerous causes of action relating to her husband's death allegedly arising out of his asbestos exposure to products manufactured by the defendant. Specifically, Plaintiff Catrett sued Defendant Celotex Corp. and others for negligence, breach of warranty, and strict liability, alleging that her husband's death was caused by exposure to asbestos products manufactured by the Celotex and the other defendants. Defendant Celotex moved for summary judgment on the grounds that plaintiff failed to produce any evidence that any Celotex product caused the injuries. In response, Catrett produced three documents which she claimed demonstrated that a genuine factual issue existed. The defendant argued that the three documents, including the husband's deposition and two letters, were inadmissible hearsay. The District Court granted the defendant's motion for summary judgment because there was no showing that the plaintiff was exposed to the defendant's product. The Court of Appeals reversed as Celotex made no effort to introduce any evidence, affidavits or otherwise, in support of its motion for summary judgment. The Supreme Court granted certiorari.

I

In a motion for summary judgment, must the moving party supply evidence or affidavits showing the absence of a genuine dispute about a material fact?

R

A moving party may meet its burden of persuasion by demonstrating that the non-moving party failed to supply sufficient evidence of a genuine dispute of material fact in a summary judgment motion.

A

The burden of supplying evidence or affidavits showing the absence of a genuine dispute about a material fact need not be shouldered by the party moving for summary judgment. FRCP Rule 56(c) mandates the entry of summary judgment, after adequate time for discovery, against a party who fails to establish the existence of an element essential to that party's case, and on which that party will hold the burden of proof at trial. The Court of Appeals misconstrued the holding of *Adickes v. S. H. Kress & Co.* (the party moving for summary judgment must establish the absence of a genuine issue, when viewed in a light most favorable to the opposing party). This holding should not be interpreted to mean that the burden is always on the moving party to produce, and in showing the absence of, a material fact in dispute. Rather, a summary judgment motion may properly be made in relying solely on the pleadings, depositions, answers to interrogatories and admissions on file. Thus, the moving party does not have to submit supporting evidence as the plain language of Rule 56(a) and (b) indicate. The moving party only bears the initial responsibility of informing the court of the basis for its motion. This responsibility may be met by

---

showing the court that there is an absence of evidence to support the nonmoving party's case.

C Reversed and remanded.

Bias v. Advantage International Inc.

905 F.2d 1558 (1990)

FACTS

Leonard K. Bias, a college basketball star at the U. of Maryland, entered into a representation agreement with defendants Advantage International, Inc. and A. Lee Fentress. Bias was later drafted in the first round by the Boston Celtics. Two days later, he died of a cocaine overdose. Bias had used cocaine in the past. Bias's estate (plaintiff) sued the defendants under a breach of contract theory for (1) not obtaining a 1 million dollar life insurance policy on his life; (2) misrepresenting that they had obtained one; and (3) in reliance on defendants' misrepresentation that they had obtained insurance coverage, Bias's parents did not secure independent insurance coverage as a result. Defendants' motioned the court for summary judgment, which was granted. Plaintiff appealed.

I

Did the moving party (plaintiff) carry its burden with respect to the motion for summary judgment?

R

Upon a motion for summary judgment, the movant bears the burden of showing of an absence of genuine issues of material fact; if he does, the nonmoving party must come forward with specific facts to demonstrate the contrary [a genuine issue for trial].

A

Upon a motion for summary judgment, the movant bears the burden of showing of an absence of genuine issues of material fact; if he does, the nonmoving party must come forward with specific facts to demonstrate the contrary – that a genuine issue for trial exists. Here, the district court based its decision upon a finding that there was no genuine issue of material fact with regard to Bias's insurability rested on two conclusions: (1) Bias was a drug user; and (2) Bias could not have obtained a life insurance policy because he was a drug user. As to the first issue, the defendants offered the eyewitness testimony stating that Bias had used cocaine on numerous occasions prior to his death. In response, the estate offered general statements – it did not impeach the defendants' witnesses and failed to contradict the specific testimony evidence presented. Without direct evidence to the contrary, there is no genuine issue of material fact as to Bias's past drug use. With respect to (2), concerning the availability of a life insurance policy, the defendants offered evidence that ***every*** insurance company questioned an applicant's present/past drug use at some point in the process. In response, the estate offered some general evidence to the contrary, but it failed to come proffer ***specific facts*** to demonstrate that some insurance company would have insured Bias without inquiring about his past drug use. Consequently, the defendants met their burden of demonstrating an absence of a genuine issue of material fact, and the plaintiff failed to assert specific facts in rebuttal.

C

Summary judgment was appropriate in this case. Affirmed.

Sanders v. Union Pacific Railroad Co.

U.S. Court of Appeals, 154 F.2d 1037 (9th Cir. 1998)

FACTS

In June 1995, plaintiff Phillip Sanders sued his employer, defendant Union Pacific Railroad Co., under the Federal Employer's Liability Act, following a work-related back injury. The district judge set a trial date for November 19, 1996 and a pretrial conference for November 8 and issued a form order concerning preparation for the conference. The order set forth a schedule for the filing of motions, oppositions, proposed instructions, and other documents and warned that failure to comply would lead to sanctions or dismissal. Plaintiff's counsel failed to comply with any of the requirements of the order. He consistently submitted documents late and failed to submit a trial brief. At the pretrial conference, plaintiff's counsel explained that his responsibilities in another matter lasted longer than he anticipated and, as a result, he was unable to meet his current deadlines imposed by the judge in this case. The clerk at the conference indicated that the case would be removed from the calendar and that the judge would likely take other action. However, one week later the court dismissed plaintiff's action with prejudice.

I Does a court abuse its discretion when it dismisses an action with prejudice for failure to obey an order when lesser sanctions are available?

R A court may dismiss an action for prejudice, in its own discretion, if a party's failure to comply with deadlines and court orders leads to unnecessary delay and expense without considering lesser sanctions, even if such sanctions are readily available.

A Here, plaintiff's counsel's repeated failures undoubtedly impaired defendant Union Pacific's ability to prepare for trial. He did not inform the court of his inability to meet impending deadlines. By not doing so, plaintiff's counsel deprived the court of the opportunity to impose lesser sanctions. Public policy is also impacted – an increase in delay and expense threatens to overwhelm our courts. There was no abuse of discretion by the district court. The dismissal was entered by the court *sua sponte*, which means that counsel should have been warned that a dismissal was immanent. As such, we reject plaintiff's contention that the dismissal violated the Due Process Clause.

C We affirm.

McKey v. Fairbairn

345 F.2d 739 (D.C. Cir. 1965)

FACTS

Mrs. Littlejohn, a tenant, notified her landlord, one Fairbairn, of a leak in a room in her apartment. Before he could fix it, an all-night rain fell and caused the floor to become wet. Shortly thereafter, Mrs. Littlejohn entered the room to clean the mess with a mop and then left. She returned a short time later, slipped and fell, and sustained injuries as a result. She then sued for negligence, but died from causes unrelated to the fall before the end of trial. Plaintiff Helen McKey, her administratrix, was substituted as plaintiff. The pretrial order contained plaintiff's theory of the case. It stated that Littlejohn's injuries were a result of Fairbairn's negligence in failing to repair the roof and eliminate the leak after he was given notice and after he promised to repair it. This, plaintiff claimed, constituted a breach of a duty owed under the lease. During the trial plaintiff's attorney became aware of housing regulations requiring roofs to be leak-proof and thus moved to amend the pretrial order to allow this information into evidence. The court denied the motion and directed verdict for defendant.

I

Does a court abuse its discretion when it refuses to allow a party to amend the pretrial order to allow in pertinent evidence relevant to its claims?

R

A trial judge has great discretion to legitimately and properly refuse to allow a party to amend its pretrial order.

A

A trial judge has great discretion to legitimately and properly refuse to allow a party to amend its pretrial order. We do not address whether proffered housing regulations are germane to the instant case since the trail judge acted within his discretion in refusing to admit it. Also, since Mrs. Littlejohn admitted she knew of the floor was wet and yet failed exercise proper care, the trial judge would have been justified in instructing the jury that she was contributorily negligent as a matter of law.

C

Affirmed.

Reid v. San Pedro, Los Angeles & Salt Lake RR

39 Utah 617, 118 P. 1009 (1911)

FACTS

Plaintiff Reid filed suit against defendant San Pedro, Los Angeles & Salt Lake Railroad to recover damages for the killing of her cattle by defendant's train. Plaintiff argued that the Railroad negligently maintained the fence along the railroad which was broken and in disrepair and down in certain areas. This negligence, plaintiff contends, allowed her cattle easy passage through the same and onto the railroad tracts where one was killed by a passing train. Plaintiff kept the cattle on private land owned by another and located next to the train tracks behind some gates. It was not argued at trial that Railroad left the gates open. Rather, the evidence showed that the animal was killed in the immediate vicinity of the open gate and about a mile from the downed portion of the fence. No direct evidence was offered as to how the animal actually reached the tracks. Nor was there any evidence that the train was operated negligently. The jury returned a verdict in favor of plaintiff and defendant appealed based upon insufficient evidence to support the verdict.

I

Where liability is established based upon two equal inferences [broken fence or open gates], one which could establish liability and the other which could not, does sufficient evidence exist to support a verdict?

R

A plaintiff cannot meet her burden of proof to establish liability by a preponderance of the evidence where there are two equal inferences, only one of which can establish liability [i.e., the evidence will not support a verdict].

A

Defendant-railroad asserts on appeal that there is insufficient evidence to support the verdict because it cannot be determined how the cattle got onto the tracks. Statutory law provides that whenever a railroad company provides gates at private crossings for the convenience of the land owners, the gates must be closed at all times when not in use, and if the owner fails to do so, and his animals stray onto the tracks, the owner cannot recover damages for killed or injured animals. Defendant-railroad argues that since the cattle could have passed through the open gate and onto the tracks, precluding liability, the verdict must be set aside. Yet there was no direct evidence as to how the cattle got onto the tracks, and a strong inference also exists that the animal entered through the gate. It is the plaintiff who holds the affirmative burden of proof to establish liability by a preponderance of the evidence. It is a familiar rule that where there are two equal inferences, one which establishes liability and the other which does not, the plaintiff has not met his burden. Such is the case before us. The plaintiff failed to prove otherwise and thus the verdict is not supported by the evidence.

C

The trial court should have directed a verdict for the Railroad.

Chauffeurs, Teamsters & Helpers, Local No. 391 v. Terry

U.S. Supreme Court, 494 U.S. 558 (1990)

FACTS

Teamsters filed suit against their Union alleging violations of fair representation by the Union. Mclean Trucking Co. and the Chauffeurs, Teamsters and Defendant Helpers Local 391 (Union) were parties to a collective bargaining agreement. Plaintiff Terry and 26 other plaintiffs were employed by Mclean as truck drivers and were all members of the Union. Plaintiff Terry and the others filed a grievance with the Union, but the Union declined to refer the claim to a grievance committee. The plaintiff and the other employees then filed suit in District Court alleging the Union had violated its duty of fair representation. The Union moved to strike the plaintiff's request for a jury trial on the grounds that no right to a jury trial existed in a duty of fair representation suit. The District Court denied the motion to strike and the Fourth Circuit Affirmed upon an interlocutory appeal. The Supreme Court of the United States granted certiorari.

I

Where there has been an alleged breach of fair representation by a union, does a union member seeking an award have a right to a trial by a jury?

R

An action for a breach of fair representation by a union allows for a jury trial.

A

An action for a breach of fair representation by a union allows for a jury trial. Therefore, a union member seeking an award of back pay from the Union's alleged breach of fair representation ***does*** have a right to a trial by a jury. In order to determine whether a particular action involved legal rights, and hence whether a jury trial is allowed, we conduct a two step analysis: (1) we compare the statutory action to the 18th century English actions which existed prior to the merger of law and equity; then (2) we look at the remedy requested to determine whether its equitable or legal in nature. With respect to step (1) above, causes of action for breach of a union's duty of fair representation did not exist in 18th century England. However, we are persuaded by the Union's analogy between a duty of fair representation action and an action by a beneficiary against a trustee for breach of a fiduciary duty. With respect to step (2), we note that the only remedy sought by Plaintiff Terry is an award of back pay and benefits. While this award is for compensatory damages, we are not of the opinion that awards of monetary relief must always be legal in nature. Thus, we hold that the award of back pay is legal in nature and not a form of restitutionary relief. Thus, the right to a jury trial is upheld.

C

Affirmed.

Amoco Oil Co. v. Torcomian

722 F.2d 1099 (3rd Cir. 1983)

FACTS

Defendant Torcomian appeals from a judgment denying him the right to a jury trial on the claim by plaintiff Amoco Oil Co. against him and his compulsory counterclaim against the plaintiff. The basis for the lower court's denial of his request for a jury trial was that the claims were allegedly equitable in nature; stemming from a dispute between the parties involving a service station owned by Amoco and to be run by defendant under a franchise agreement. Plaintiff initially sued assert numerous claims, but at the beginning of trial, it attempted to orally amend its complaint to delete portions of its complaint that sought money damages, other than for *mesne* [in the middle; between two extremes] profits. Plaintiff purposely did so to foreclose defendant's right to jury trial. Defendant had filed a counterclaim against Amoco seeking an injunction and money damages for lost profits, fraud, and attorneys' fees. A bench trial occurred and the defendant lost. Defendant appealed contending that its counterclaim contained legal claims which should have afforded it a jury trial.

I

Does a complaint requesting both equitable relief and legal relief foreclose the right to a jury trial?

R

Seeking equitable relief in addition to legal relief does not eliminate the right to a jury trial.

A

The joinder of an equitable claim with a legal claim does not foreclose the right to a jury trial. With respect to defendant's counterclaim, it sought both equitable relief and money damages for the past breach of contract. For that reason, a jury trial should have been granted ***unless*** the error was harmless. Here, the error was not harmless. An error is considered harmless if a plaintiff would have been entitled to a directed verdict anyway. Since the nature of the claims was based largely on issues of credibility, a directed verdict could not have been properly granted on either the claim or counterclaim. Accordingly, defendant was entitled to a jury trial under the 7th Amendment.

C

Judgment vacated and case remanded for a new trial.

In re Boston's Children First

244 F.3d 164 (1st Cir. 2001)

FACTS

The plaintiffs challenged Boston's elementary school assignment process, claiming that they had been denied preferred school assignments on the basis of their race, in violation of state and federal law. Judge Gertner gave the plaintiffs the option of a court ruling on the plaintiffs' pending motion for a preliminary injunction at the time of the motion or suspending a ruling pending further discovery. The plaintiffs chose the latter option. Thereafter, in a newspaper article, the plaintiffs' counsel criticized the decision not to issue a preliminary injunction, stating that her decision was in conflict with a prior decision [the Mack case]. In the *Mack* case, the judge granted a preliminary judgment in a matter involving the strip search of female jail inmates. Judge Gertner responded ***publicly*** to what she viewed as inaccuracies in the article and commented on the complexities of the case. Based on her comments, the plaintiffs moved for recusal because her "impartiality might reasonably be questioned." Judge Gertner refused to recuse herself and the plaintiffs requested a writ of mandamus from the Court of Appeals directing the judge to recuse herself.

I

Should a sitting judge recuse herself after publicly commenting on a pending case?

R

Only when an accusation of bias or prejudice is supported by some factual basis that objectively and reasonably places a judge's impartiality in question, is recusal appropriate.

A

Under §455(a), a judge must disqualify herself "in any proceeding in which [her] impartiality might reasonably be questioned." The statute does not, however, give litigants free reign to demand recusal of a judge for any reason. Only when an accusation of bias or prejudice is supported by some factual basis that objectively and reasonably places a judge's impartiality in question, is recusal appropriate. In the instant case, the plaintiff's main contention is that Judge Gertner's comment that the present case is "more complex" than *Mack* suggests that the plaintiffs' claims lacked merit and were unlikely to be upheld. Canon 3(A)(6) of the Code of Judicial Conduct instructs that a judge should speak publicly on the merits of a pending matter, except for public statements made in the course of the judge's official duties, to explain court procedures, or for educational purposes. The infusion of race-based issues surrounding school assignments was subject to heightened media attention, so Judge Gertner's general comments can be construed as more inflammatory under the circumstances, creating the appearance of impropriety.

C

Even though no actual bias may exist, Judge Gertner must recuse herself. Writ granted.

Thompson v. Altheimer & Gray

248 F.3d 621 (7th Cir. 2003)

FACTS

Plaintiff Thompson sued her employer, defendant Altheimer & Gray, for racial discrimination under Title VII of the Civil Rights Act of 1964. After the case was tried and a verdict was returned in favor of the defendant, the plaintiff appealed, alleging a juror named Leiter should have been stricken for cause [if the plaintiff is correct in her assertion, she would be entitled to a new trial]. During voir dire, Leiter informed the judge that as a business owner, her decision would be swayed toward the defendant. Leiter also informed the judge that she would do her best, but that her experience would most likely cloud her judgment. She also stated that she believed that sometimes employees file bogus lawsuits simply because they haven't gotten a promotion or a raise or some other benefit. Notwithstanding the foregoing, Leiter promised to be as fair as she could. Subsequently, the court denied the plaintiff's request to strike Leiter for cause and the jury was impaneled. Each juror, including Leiter, positively indicated that he or she would follow the judge's instruction on the law even if they didn't agree with them and would suspend judgment until all evidence had been considered.

I Should a juror be stricken for cause after expressing a belief that might favor one side or the other while simultaneously promising to be fair, to uphold the law and suspend judgment until all evidence had been considered?

R A juror should be stricken for cause when he/she demonstrates bias against any party.

A When a juror expresses a patent bias against any party, that juror should be stricken for cause and replaced with an alternate. The expression of a true, realistic belief, however, does not evidence bias *per se*. In this case, Leiter expressed a belief that sometimes employees file bogus lawsuits simply because they haven't gotten a promotion or a raise or some other benefit. This belief, standing in isolation, does not in of itself establish bias without probing further – would such a belief impair the juror's judgment? No such inquiry was made here. Here, the judge asked the entire jury if it could be faithful to his instructions, but did not seek individual assurances from each juror to uncover any potential bias.

C Reversed and remanded for a new trial.

Pennsylvania Railroad v. Chamberlain

U.S. Supreme Court, 288 U.S. 333 (1933)

FACTS

This is an action brought by respondent against petitioner to recover for the death of a brakeman, alleged to have been caused by petitioner's negligence. The complaint alleges that the deceased, at the time of the accident resulting in his death, was assisting in the yard work of breaking up and making up trains and in the classifying and assorting of cars operating in interstate commerce; that in pursuance of such work, while riding a cut of cars, other cars ridden by fellow employees were negligently caused to be brought into violent contact with those upon which deceased was riding, with the result that he was thrown therefrom to the railroad track and run over by a car or cars, inflicting injuries from which he died. At the conclusion of the evidence, the trial court directed the jury to find a verdict in favor of petitioner. Judgment upon a verdict so found was reversed by the Court of Appeals.

I

Where the facts give rise to and support two inconsistent inferences, has a party sustained his burden of proving facts by a preponderance of the evidence?

R

Where the facts give rise to and support two inconsistent inferences, a party has not sustained his burden of proving facts by a preponderance of the evidence.

A

The case for respondent rests wholly upon the claim that the fall of deceased was caused by a violent collision of the string of nine cars with the string ridden by deceased. Three employees, riding the nine-car string, testified positively that no such collision occurred. They were corroborated by every other employee in a position to see, all testifying that there was no contact between the nine-car string and that of the deceased. The testimony of these witnesses, if believed, establishes beyond doubt that there was no collision between these two strings of cars, and that the nine-car string contributed in no way to the accident. The only witness who testified for the respondent was one Bainbridge; and it is upon his testimony alone that respondent's right to recover is sought to be upheld. It, of course, is true, generally, that where there is a direct conflict of testimony upon a matter of fact, the question must be left to the jury to determine, without regard to the number of witnesses upon either side. But here there really is no conflict in the testimony as to the facts. The witnesses for petitioner flatly testified that there was no collision between the nine-car and the two-car strings. Bainbridge did not say there was such a collision. What he said was that he heard a 'loud crash,' which did not cause him at once to turn, but that shortly thereafter he did turn and saw the two strings of cars moving together with the deceased no longer in sight; that there was nothing unusual about the crash of cars-it happened every day; that there was nothing about this crash to attract his attention except that it was extra loud; that he paid no attention to it; that it was not sufficient to attract his attention. There is no direct evidence that in fact the crash was occasioned by a collision of the two strings in question; and it is perfectly clear that no such fact was brought to Bainbridge's attention as a perception of the physical sense of sight or of hearing. At most there was an inference to that effect drawn from observed facts which gave equal support to the opposite inference that the crash was occasioned by the coming together of other strings of cars entirely away from the scene of the accident, or of the two-car string ridden by deceased and the seven-car string immediately ahead of it. We, therefore, have a case belonging to that class of cases where proven facts give equal support to each of two inconsistent inferences; in which event, neither of them being established, judgment, as a matter of law, must go against the party upon whom rests the necessity of sustaining one of these inferences as against the other, before he is entitled to recover. The rule is succinctly stated in *Smith v. First National Bank in Westfield*: "There being several inferences deducible from the facts which appear, and equally consistent with all those facts, the plaintiff has not maintained the proposition upon which alone he would be entitled to recover. There is strictly no evidence to warrant a jury in finding that the loss was occasioned by negligence and not by theft. When the evidence tends equally to sustain either of two inconsistent propositions, neither of them can be said to have been established by legitimate proof. A verdict in favor of the party bound to maintain one of those propositions against the other is necessarily wrong." Not only is Bainbridge's testimony considered as a whole suspicious, insubstantial, and insufficient, but his statement that when he turned shortly after hearing the crash the two strings were moving together is simply incredible, if he meant thereby to be understood as saying that he saw the two in contact; and if he meant by the words 'moving together' simply that they were moving at the same time in the same direction but not in contact, the statement becomes immaterial. We think, therefore, that the trial court was right in withdrawing the case from the jury. It repeatedly has been held by this court that before evidence may be left to the jury, there is a preliminary question for the judge, not whether there is literally no evidence, but whether there is any upon which a jury can properly proceed to find a verdict for the party producing it, upon whom the onus of proof is imposed. The rule is settled for the federal courts, and for many of the state courts, that whenever in the trial of a civil case the evidence is clearly such that if a verdict were rendered for one of the parties the other would be entitled to a new trial, it is the duty of the judge to direct the jury to find according to the views of the court. Such a practice, this court has said, not only saves time and expense, but gives scientific certainty to the law in its application to the facts and promotes the ends of justice.

C

The judgment of the Circuit Court of Appeals is reversed and that of the District Court is affirmed.

Lind v. Schenley Industries

278 F.2d 79 (3d Cir. 1960)

FACTS

Plaintiff Lind, a sales manager for defendant-liquor company, sued the latter for breach of oral contract. Plaintiff and his secretary testified as to certain promises made by the defendant, Schenley Industries, and agents for defendant testified to the contrary. The jury found a contract existed and an award in the plaintiff's favor followed. The trial judge granted defendant's j.n.o.v. motion and, in the alternative, a new trial. The district court granted the alternative a motion for a new trial because it found the jury's verdict (1) contrary to the weight of the evidence, (2) contrary to law and (3) a result of error in the admission of evidence. Plaintiff appealed.

I

Does a trial judge abuse his discretion when he substitutes his judgment for that of the jury concerning the weight of the evidence when granting a new trial?

R

A trial judge abuses his discretion in granting a new trial where he substitutes his judgment for that of the jury concerning the weight of the evidence.

A

A trial judge abuses his discretion in granting a new trial where he substitutes his judgment for that of the jury concerning the weight of the evidence. In order to overturn such a grant, there must be a clear showing that the trial judge abused his discretion. As long as an appellate court believes that injustice may result, it may reverse the lower court. That said, a trial judge has broad discretion in deciding whether or not a new trial should be granted; however, but he may not set aside the jury's verdict simply because he would have decided the case differently than that of the jury. We thus conclude that the trial judge substituted his judgment for that of the jury and therefore abused his legal discretion. We reverse and remand the case with direction to reinstate the verdict and judgment in favor of plaintiff.

C

Reversed and remanded.

Peterson v. Wilson

141 F.3d 573 (5th Cir. 1998)

FACTS

Plaintiff Peterson sued for federal statutory and constitutional claims under 42 U.S.C. §§ 1983 and 1988 after being fired from Texas Southern University where he worked as a grant director claiming he was "arbitrarily and capriciously terminated." The jury returned a verdict in plaintiff's favor and he was awarded damages. Following the verdict, defendant Wilson, renewed his motion for a j.n.o.v. and supplemented it with an alternative motion for new trial. Four months later, the Magistrate judge granted the new trial "based on the jury's verdict and *comments the jurors made to the court after returning the verdict* [and outside the presence of the parties and their respective counsel], that the jury completely disregarded the Court's instructions. Instead, it appears that the jury considered improper factors in reaching its verdict. Accordingly, the Court deems it in the interest of justice to grant a new trial." Plaintiff unsuccessfully moved for reconsideration and the case was re-tried and a jury verdict was rendered in favor of defendant. Plaintiff appealed.

I

Is it error to grant a new trial based upon post-verdict statements from jurors relating to their deliberations?

R

The granting of a new trial based upon post verdict statements from jurors relating to their deliberations is improper.

A

The granting of a new trial based upon post verdict statements from jurors relating to their deliberations is improper. The trial judge relied upon information he obtained from the jurors after the verdict and outside the presence of the parties and counsel to grant a new trial. This is not permitted. Rule 606(b) provides that when inquiring into the validity of a verdict, a juror may not testify concerning matters or statements made during the jury's deliberations, such as another juror's mind or emotions influencing a juror to vote a certain way, or the mental processes involved in the deliberations, except that a jury may testify on the question of whether extraneous prejudicial information or outside influence which was improperly brought to the jury's attention. Moreover, juror testimony may not be used to impeach a jury verdict. In *Robles v. Exxon Corp.* we held that receiving testimony from jurors after they had returned their verdict, for the purpose of ascertaining whether the jury misunderstood the jury instructions is prohibited by Rule 606(b). We therefore must reverse the trial court's grant of a new trial, vacate the court's judgment rendered on the basis of the jury verdict in the second trial, and reinstate the results of the first trial.

C

We thus remand the case to the district court for entry of judgment in favor of plaintiff and against defendant.

Liberty Mutual Insurance Co. v. Wetzel

U.S. Supreme Court, 424 U.S. 737 (1976)

FACTS

The plaintiff sued the defendant in federal court alleging that the defendant's employee insurance benefits and maternity leave provisions violated Title VII of the Civil Rights Act of 1964. Plaintiff (Wetzel) sought a declaratory judgment, an injunction and damages. The District Court granted Wetzel partial summary judgment on the issue of liability, holding that the policies did violate Title VII. However, the judgment did not provide any relief sought by the plaintiff. Defendant Liberty Mutual appealed the grant of partial summary judgment and the Third Circuit held that it had jurisdiction and affirmed the judgment. The Supreme Court of the United States granted certiorari.

I

May a Court of Appeals review the District Court's decision to grant partial summary judgment?

R

Partial summary judgment on the issue of liability is an interlocutory order and is not appealable.

A

A Court of Appeals does not have jurisdiction to review the District Court's decision to grant partial summary judgment. Such orders are interlocutory in nature, and thus are not final judgments within the meaning of 28 U.S.C. §1291. Thus it is not applicable as a basis for jurisdiction in the instant action. If the District Court had granted injunctive relief, this interlocutory order would have been appealable under §1292(a)(1). However, when it decided the issue of the defendant's liability, the District Court granted no relief whatsoever. Moreover, Rule 54(b) does not apply to cases like this, which are actions on a single claim and the requirement of §1292(b) was not satisfied. If this Court were to allow the Court of Appeals to exercise jurisdiction over cases like these, we would condone the procedure whereby any District Court could render an interlocutory decision on a liability issue rendering it immediately appealable.

C

No. A Court of Appeals does not have jurisdiction to review a District Court's order granting partial summary judgment on the issue of liability.

Lauro Lines s.r.l. v. Chasser

U.S. Supreme Court, 490 U.S. 495 (1989)

FACTS

Respondents - passengers and representatives of the estates of passengers on a cruise ship hijacked by terrorists - filed suit in the District Court against petitioner, the ship's owner, to recover damages for personal injuries and for the wrongful death of one passenger. Before trial, petitioner moved to dismiss the actions, citing the forum-selection clause printed on each passenger ticket, which purported to obligate passengers to institute any suit in connection with the contract in Italy and to renounce the right to sue elsewhere. The District Court denied the motions, holding that the ticket did not give passengers reasonable notice that they were waiving the opportunity to sue in a domestic forum. The Court of Appeals dismissed petitioner's appeal on the ground that the District Court's dismissal orders were interlocutory and not appealable under 28 U.S.C. 1291, holding that the orders did not fall within the exception to the rule of non-appealability carved out by the collateral order doctrine.

I

Is an interlocutory order denying a defendant's motion to dismiss a damages action on the basis of a contractual forum-selection clause immediately appealable under 1291?

R

An interlocutory order denying a defendant's motion to dismiss a damages action on the basis of a contractual forum-selection clause is not immediately appealable under 1291.

A

An interlocutory order denying a defendant's motion to dismiss a damages action on the basis of a contractual forum-selection clause is not immediately appealable under 1291. Such an order is not final in the usual sense, for it does not end the litigation on the merits but, on the contrary, ensures that the litigation will continue. Nor does the order fall within the narrow exception to the normal application of the final judgment rule known as the collateral order doctrine, for the order is not effectively unreviewable on appeal from final judgment. The right to be sued only in a particular forum, as compared to the right to avoid suit altogether, although not perfectly secured by an appeal after final judgment, is sufficiently vindicable at that stage and is not essentially destroyed if vindication is postponed until trial is completed. That there may be a policy favoring enforcement of foreign forum-selection clauses goes to the merits of petitioner's claim that its ticket agreement requires that suit be filed in Italy and that the agreement should be enforced by the federal courts, but does not affect the appealability of a prejudgment order, which turns on the right asserted, not on the likelihood of eventual success on the merits.

C

Affirmed.

Anderson v. Bessemer City

U.S. Supreme Court, 470 U.S. 564 (1985)

FACTS

In 1975, respondent city set about to hire a new Recreation Director to manage the city's recreational facilities and to develop recreational programs. A committee, consisting of four men and one woman, was responsible for choosing the Director. Eight persons applied for the position, including petitioner, the only woman applicant. At the time, petitioner was a 39-year-old schoolteacher with college degrees in social studies and education. The committee offered the position to a 24-year-old male applicant, who had recently graduated from college with a degree in physical education. The four men on the committee voted to offer the job to him, and only the woman voted for petitioner. Petitioner then filed discrimination charges with the Equal Employment Opportunity Commission (EEOC), which, upon finding that there was reasonable cause to believe that petitioner's charges were true, invited the parties to engage in conciliation proceedings. When these efforts proved unsuccessful, the EEOC issued petitioner a right-to-sue letter, and she filed an action in Federal District Court under Title VII of the Civil Rights Act of 1964. After a trial in which testimony from petitioner, the applicant who was hired, and members of the selection committee was heard, the court issued a memorandum announcing its finding that petitioner was entitled to judgment because she had been denied the position on account of her sex. The memorandum requested petitioner to submit proposed findings of fact and conclusions of law expanding upon those set forth in the memorandum. When petitioner complied with this request, the court requested and received a response setting forth respondent's objections to the proposed findings. The court then issued its own findings of fact and conclusions of law. The court's finding that petitioner had been denied employment because of her sex was based on findings of fact that she was the most qualified candidate, that she had been asked questions during her interview regarding her spouse's feelings about her application for the position that other applicants were not asked, and that the male committee members were biased against hiring a woman. The Court of Appeals reversed, holding that the District Court's findings were clearly erroneous and that the court had therefore erred in finding that petitioner had been discriminated against on account of sex.

I

Must an appellate court conduct a de novo review when reviewing findings of fact?

R

An appellate court must use a "clearly erroneous" standard and not conduct a de novo review when reviewing findings of fact.

A

The Court of Appeals misapprehended and misapplied the clearly-erroneous standard and accordingly erred in denying petitioner relief under Title VII. Where the District Court did not simply adopt petitioner's proposed findings but provided respondent with an opportunity to respond to those findings and the findings ultimately issued varied considerably from those proposed by petitioner, there is no reason to doubt that the ultimate findings represented the court's own considered conclusions or to subject those findings to a more stringent appellate review than is called for by the applicable rules. Under Federal Rule of Civil Procedure 52(a) - which provides that "[f]indings of fact shall not be set aside unless clearly erroneous, and due regard shall be given to the opportunity of the trial court to judge of the credibility of the witness" - "[a] finding is `clearly erroneous' when although there is evidence to support it, the reviewing court on the entire evidence is left with a definite and firm conviction that a mistake has been committed." *United States v. United States Gypsum Co.* If the district court's account of the evidence is plausible in light of the record viewed in its entirety, the court of appeals may not reverse it even though convinced that had it been sitting as the trier of fact, it would have weighed the evidence differently. This is so even when the district court's findings do not rest on credibility determinations, but are based on physical or documentary evidence or inferences from other facts. When findings are based on determinations regarding the credibility of witnesses, Rule 52(a) demands even greater deference to the trial court's finding. Application of the above principles to the facts of this case discloses that the Court of Appeals erred in its employment of the clearly-erroneous standard. The District Court's finding that petitioner was better qualified was entitled to deference notwithstanding it was not based on credibility determinations, and the record contains nothing that mandates a holding that the finding was clearly erroneous. As to the District Court's finding that petitioner was the only applicant asked questions regarding her spouse's feelings about her application for the position, the Court of Appeals erred in failing to give due regard to the District Court's ability to interpret and discern the credibility of oral testimony, especially that of the woman member of the selection committee, whose testimony the District Court felt supported the finding. Given that that finding was not clearly erroneous, the District Court's finding of bias cannot be termed erroneous. It is supported not only by the treatment of petitioner in her interview but also by the testimony of one committee member that he believed it would have been difficult for a woman to perform the job and by evidence that another member solicited applications only from men. Because the findings on which the District Court based its finding of sex discrimination were not clearly erroneous, its finding of discrimination was also not clearly erroneous.

C

Reversed.

Harnden v. Jayco Inc.

496 F.3d 579 (6th Cir. 2007)

FACTS

Plaintiff Glenn Harnden bought a Jayco Eagle Recreational Vehicle. He returned it several times for repair of defects, but the defects were never fixed. He filed a complaint against defendant Jayco Inc., the manufacturer, for breach of contract, violation of the Michigan Consumer Protection Act, breach of written warranty, revocation of acceptance, breach of implied warranty, breach of express warranty, breach of implied warranty of merchantability, and violation of the Michigan Motor Vehicle Service and Repair Act of 2004. An expert report prepared by Randy Zonker, a Jayco employee, determined the problems were only minor and did not stem from the manufacturer, and Harnden did not rebut Zonker's conclusions. The district court granted Jayco summary judgment. On appeal, Harnden's attorney objected to the admission of the expert report because it was not in the form of an affidavit or sworn statement as required by Federal Rule of Civil Procedure 56(e), and was therefore inadmissible hearsay.

I Is the admission of an expert report harmless error where the opposing party knew the contents of the report, and remanding the case would result only in a change in format of the report?

R The admission of an expert report is harmless error where the opposing party knew the contents of the report, and remanding the case would result only in a change in format of the report.

A Yes. The admission of an expert report is harmless error where the opposing party knew the contents of the report, and remanding the case would result only in a change in format of the report. The admission of Zonker's report is harmless because it does not affect Harnden's substantial rights. Harnden always knew of the contents of the report, and could have rebutted it, but did not.

C See above.

Frier v. City of Vandalia

770 F.2d 699 (7th Cir. 1985)

FACTS

Plaintiff Charles Frier, a citizen of defendant-city Vandalia, had a habit of parking his cars illegally on a narrow street, which forced others to drive on another citizen's lawn in order to get past plaintiff's car. During 1983, the police had four of plaintiff's cars towed to various garages in the city. Plaintiff balked at paying the $10 garage fee, and instead filed suits in Illinois state court seeking replevin. In each suit plaintiff named as defendants both the City of Vandalia (defendant) and the garage that had towed the car. One of the suits was voluntarily dismissed when plaintiff got his cars back; the two other cases were consolidated and litigated. Plaintiff's writ of replevin was denied in each case. After losing in state court, plaintiff turned to federal court, arguing that defendant had not offered him a hearing either before or after it took the cars and that it is the "official policy" of the defendant not to do so. The complaint invoked the Due Process Clause and 42 U.S.C. § 1983, and it sought equitable relief in addition to $100,000.00 in compensatory and $100,000.00 in punitive damages. The district court dismissed plaintiff complaint for failure to state a claim on which relief may be granted. Plaintiff appealed.

I

Does the law of preclusion [also called res judicata or estoppel by judgment] apply? or stated another way, can a plaintiff bring the same suit against the same defendant more than once?

R

One suit precludes a second where the parties and the cause of action are identical.

A

A court ought not resolve a constitutional dispute unless that is absolutely necessary. Here it is not. Here it is not. Plaintiff had his day in court in the replevin action. The district court bypassed this argument because, it believed, plaintiff could not have asserted his constitutional arguments in a replevin action. This is only partially correct. Plaintiff could not have obtained punitive damages or declaratory relief in a suit limited to replevin. But he was free to join one count seeking such relief with another seeking replevin. As such, the law of Illinois, which governs the preclusive effect to be given to the judgment in the replevin actions, would bar this suit. Defendant is therefore entitled to prevail on the ground of claim preclusion, although the district court did not decide the case on that ground. Illinois recognizes the principles of claim preclusion, also called res judicata or estoppel by judgment. Under that doctrine, one suit precludes a second where the parties and the cause of action are identical. Causes of action are identical where the evidence necessary to sustain a second verdict would sustain the first, i.e., where the causes of action are based on a common core of operative facts. Two suits may entail the same cause of action even though they present different legal theories, and the first suit operates as an absolute bar to a subsequent action, not only as to every matter which was offered and received to sustain or defeat the claim or demand, but as to any other admissible matter which might have been offered for that purpose. In this case the defendant was a defendant in each replevin action. Plaintiff could have urged constitutional grounds as reasons for replevin. He also could have joined a constitutional claim seeking punitive damages and declaratory relief to his demand for replevin, and therefore he had a full and fair opportunity to litigate. The actions also involve both the same common core of operative facts and the same transactions. The replevin actions diverged from the path of this § 1983 suit only because the state judge adjudicated on the merits the proprlety of the seizures. Having found the seizures proper, the judge had no occasion to determine whether the defendant should have offered plaintiff an earlier hearing. But this divergence does not mean that the two causes of action require a different core of operative facts. The final question is whether it makes a difference that only two of the replevin actions went to judgment, while here plaintiff challenges the towing of four cars. Under Illinois law the answer is no. The defendant may invoke claim preclusion when the plaintiff litigated in the first suit a subset of all available disputes between the parties. If plaintiff had filed the current suit in state court, he would have lost under the doctrine of claim preclusion. Under 28 U.S.C. § 1738, which requires federal courts to follow state claim preclusion rules, he therefore loses in federal court as well.

C

Affirmed.

Martino v. McDonald's System Inc.

598 F.2d 1079 (7th Cir. 1979), cert. denied.

FACTS

In 1962, plaintiff Martino and his brothers entered into a franchise and lease agreement with defendant McDonald's Systems Inc. for the operation of a McDonald's restaurant in Ottumwa. Iowa. The contract provided that neither plaintiff nor a member of his immediate family would acquire a financial interest in a competing business without written consent from defendant. However, six years later, plaintiff's son purchased a Burger Chef franchise in Pittsburg, Kansas. Plaintiff financed this transaction. On the basis of this transaction, defendant brought suit for breach of contract. The lawsuit, which began in 1972, ended in 1973 with a consent judgment to which the district court appended findings of fact and conclusions of law. The court order also provided that the parties had entered into an agreement for the sale of the McDonald's restaurant back to defendant for $140,000.00, which was consummated. In 1975, plaintiff brought suit alleging that enforcement of the restrictions on acquisition in the original agreement violated Section 1 of the Sherman Act. The district court entered summary judgment against plaintiff on Count I of his complaint, and he appealed.

I Does a consent judgment prevent an earlier judgment from having a res judicata effect; or, stated another way, is a prior consent judgment an adjudication on the merits?

R A prior consent judgment is an adjudication on the merits - res judicata treats a judgment on the merits as an absolute bar to re-litigation between parties and those in privity with them of every matter offered and received to sustain or defeat the claim or demand and to every matter which might have been received for that purpose.

A Defendant argues that the district court correctly held that Count I of plaintiff's complaint is precluded by FRCP 13(a). Claims not coming within the definition of "compulsory counterclaim" are lost if not raised at the proper time. Rule 13(a) provides that "a pleading shall state as a counterclaim any claim which at the time of serving the pleading the pleader has against any opposing party, if it arises out of the same transaction or occurrence that is the subject matter of the opposing party's claim and does not require for its adjudication the presence of third parties of whom the court cannot acquire jurisdiction," but does not apply unless there has been some form of pleading. Plaintiff, in the prior action, filed no pleading as defined by the FRCP. As such, Rule 13 (a) does not apply to bar plaintiff's claim. Res judicata treats a judgment on the merits as an absolute bar to re-litigation between parties and those in privity with them of every matter offered and received to sustain or defeat the claim or demand and to every matter which might have been received for that purpose. The conclusion of the earlier contract lawsuit with a consent judgment does not prevent the earlier judgment from having a res judicata effect. Having determined that the prior consent judgment is an adjudication on the merits, we conclude that this judgment precludes Count I of the antitrust action. The well-settled rule for the purpose of determining the res judicata effect of a judgment is that a cause of action comprises defenses, such as the alleged antitrust violation here, that were or might have been raised. When facts form the basis of both a defense and a counterclaim, the defendant's failure to allege these facts as a defense or a counterclaim ***does not*** preclude him from relying on those facts in an action subsequently brought by him against the plaintiff. This is because notions of judicial economy give way to fairness. However, this rule is not absolute. Both precedent and policy require that res judicata bar a counterclaim when its prosecution would nullify rights established by the prior action, as we see here. In this case, defendant has terminated and repurchased plaintiff's franchise in reliance on the trial court's 1973 judgment telling them they were justified in doing so. Now plaintiff seeks to impose significant financial liability on defendant for this action. We cannot hold that the counterclaim exception to the res judicata rule, based merely on notions of convenience, permits plaintiff here to wage this direct attack on the rights established by the prior judgment. Concluding that plaintiff's claim set forth in Count I of his complaint is a direct attack on the termination rights established in the earlier judgment, we hold that plaintiff is barred from raising that claim.

C

Affirmed.

Searle Brothers v. Searle

588 P.2d 689 (Utah 1978)

FACTS

In a divorce settlement between defendant Edlean and Woodey Searle, the court gave defendant a piece of property known as the Slaugh House, which had been recorded in Woodey's name but was considered part of the marital property. Woodey's argued that he only owned half of the property, but the entire property was nonetheless given to the defendant. The other half, he claimed, belonged to a partnership known as the Searle Brothers, the plaintiffs in this action, of which he and his sons were members. Following the divorce decree, plaintiffs brought suit seeking a return of its portion of the property, arguing that Slaugh House had been paid for with partnership funds.

I For the purposes of claim and issue preclusion, do agents and principles have any mutual or successive rights of property allowing them to be in privity with one another?

R Agents and principles do not have any mutual or successive rights of property and are not, as a consequence thereof, in privity with one another - therefore the principal is not bound by any judgment against the agent unless the principal became a party or privy thereto by actually and openly defending the action.

A A person is in privity with another when he is so identified in interest with another that he represents the same legal right as that other person; privity means one whose interest has been legally represented at the time. In general, a divorce decree, like other final judgments, is conclusive as to parties and their privies, and operates as a bar to any subsequent action. In order for res judicata to apply, both suits must involve the same parties or their privies and also the same cause of action. If the subsequent suit involves different parties, those parties cannot be bound by the prior judgment. Collateral estoppel, on the other hand, arises from a different cause of action and prevents parties or their privies from re-litigating acts and issues in a second suit that were fully litigated in the first suit. This means that the plea of collateral estoppel can be asserted only against a party in the subsequent suit who was also a party or in privity with a party in a prior suit. In determining whether collateral estoppel applies, courts consider the following four tests: (1) Was the issue decided in a prior adjudication identical with the one presented in the action in question? (2) Was there a final judgment on the merits? (3) Was the party against whom the plea is asserted a party or in privity with a party to the prior adjudication? (4) Was the issue in the first case competently, fully, and fairly litigated? Under the second test above, it is clear that the divorce decree rendered the former suit a final judgment on the merits. With respect to the third test above, it is clear that the plaintiffs were not a party to the first action; hence, the only way it can be barred from pursuing this second suit is if it were in privity with the parties to the divorce action. The legal definition of "a person in privity with another" is whether a person is so identified in interest with another that he represents the same legal right. This includes a mutual or successive relationship to rights in property. As applied to judgments or decrees of court, privity means one whose interest has been legally represented at the time. In this case, the plaintiffs' interest was neither mutual nor successive. It claims no part of the interest owned by Woodey Searle, but asserts its own independent partnership interest. The first and fourth tests previously outlined also do not permit the application of collateral estoppel in this case. The partnership interest was not legally represented in the divorce suit. Woodey B. Searle was acting in his own individual capacity as the husband of Edlean (defendant) and not as a representative of the partnership. Defendant argues that Woodey was acting as an agent for the partnership, and therefore plaintiffs are bound by the results of the prior action. However, the general rule is that agents and principals do not have any mutual or successive relationship to rights of property and are not, as a consequence, in privity with each other; therefore, a principal is not bound by any judgment obtained against an agent unless the principal became a party or privy thereto by actually and openly defending the action. Further, the right to intervene as a party in a prior suit does not bind the party in the subsequent suit where he failed to so intervene. Based on the foregoing, collateral estoppel is not available to defeat the plaintiffs'' claim. The plaintiffs cannot be bound by the decree entered in the previous suit, nor is it estopped from litigating its own claim against the property in a subsequent suit.

C

Reversed.

Gargallo v. Merrill Lynch, Pierce, Fenner & Smith

918 F.2d 658 (6th Cir. 1990)

FACTS

In 1976, plaintiff Miguel Gargalio opened a margin brokerage account with defendant Merrill Lynch, a brokerage company. He maintained that account until 1980, at which time, due to bad investments and losses, he owed defendant a debt of $17,000.00. When plaintiff refused to pay, Merrill Lynch brought suit for collection in Ohio state court. In response, plaintiff filed a counterclaim alleging, among other things, violations of federal securities laws. The state court eventually dismissed the claim with prejudice for plaintiff's refusal to comply with discovery requests and orders. Plaintiff then filed suit in federal district court, charging Merrill Lynch with violations of various securities laws. The district court dismissed the suit on res judicata grounds, finding that the issues, facts, and evidence to sustain his action were identical to the claims asserted in his counterclaim, which was dismissed with prejudice. Plaintiff appealed.

I Does a federal court have to apply state claim preclusion law in deciding whether a prior state court judgment on subject matter over which only a federal court has exclusive jurisdiction is a bar to a subsequent federal court claim upon the identical cause of action?

R A final judgment by a state court upon a cause of action over which the adjudicating court had no subject matter jurisdiction does not have claim preclusive effect in any subsequent proceedings.

A The securities law claims asserted against Merrill Lynch in this case are the same as those plaintiff previously asserted in the counterclaim he filed in state court. Ohio claim preclusion law governs the final outcome of this case. Consequently, we must decide whether the state judgment dismissing plaintiff's first lawsuit would operate as a bar, under Ohio law, to the action now under review in our federal court. In Ohio, the requirements for claim preclusion or res judicata are the same as those applicable in federal court and provide: "The doctrine of res judicata is that an existing final judgment rendered upon the merits, without fraud or collusion, by a court of competent jurisdiction, is conclusive of rights, questions and facts in issue, as to the parties and their privies, in all other actions in the same or any other judicial tribunal of concurrent jurisdiction." Under Ohio law, the dismissal with prejudice of plaintiff's state court counterclaim was a final judgment rendered on the merits. We agree with the district court that the issues, facts, and evidence to sustain this action are identical to the claims asserted in the counterclaim, and we are satisfied that the federal claim giving rise to this appeal is the same claim or cause of action asserted in prior litigation. Therefore, we have no question that Ohio claim preclusion law would bar Plaintiff's federal claim. However, the district court in which plaintiff brought his claim is not an Ohio court, but a federal tribunal. Consequently, we must decide whether a federal district court may give claim preclusive effect to an Ohio judgment regarding federal securities laws that are within the exclusive jurisdiction of the federal courts. In *Marrese v. Academy of Orthopedic*

Gargallo v. Merrill Lynch, Pierce, Fenner & Smith

918 F.2d 658 (6th Cir. 1990)

Surgeons, the U.S. Supreme Court held that the full faith and credit statute requires federal courts to determine the preclusive effect of prior state court judgments, pursuant to the law of the state in which the judgment was entered, even as to claims within the exclusive jurisdiction of the federal courts. Ohio takes the position that a judgment rendered by a court lacking subject matter jurisdiction ought not to be given preclusive effect. It seems clear, then, that in Ohio, a final judgment by a court of that state, upon a cause of action over which the adjudicating court had no subject matter jurisdiction, does not have claim preclusive effect in any subsequent proceedings. Ultimately, we hold that the Ohio court judgment dismissing plaintiff's securities law claims against Merrill Lynch may not be given claim preclusive effect in a subsequent federal court action asserting those same claims because Ohio courts would not give claim preclusive effect to a prior final judgment upon a cause of action over which the Ohio court had no subject matter jurisdiction.

C Reversed and remanded.

Illinois Central Railroad v. Parks

390 N.E.2d 1078 (1979)

FACTS

Plaintiff Jessie Parks and his wife Bertha were injured when their car, driven by plaintiff, collided with an Illinois Central Gulf Railroad (defendant) train. Both sued the defendant; Bertha recovered $30,000.00 for her injuries and received nothing for his claim of loss of services and consortium. Thereafter, he sued defendant for his own injuries in a separate action. The trial court held that plaintiff's claim was not barred by the doctrine of claim preclusion and additionally held that the prior suit did not establish that plaintiff was contributorily negligent. Defendant-railroad appealed.

I

Can a plaintiff's claim be barred under a theory of issue preclusion if it raises one of two issues previously determined in a prior case where it is not clear upon which of the two issues the prior court decided the case?

R

Where a judgment may have been based upon either or any of two or more distinct facts, a party desiring to plead the judgment as an estoppel by verdict or finding upon the particular fact involved in a subsequent suit must show that it was previously decided upon that fact, or else the question will be open to a new contention.

A

When a prior case was determined on one of two separate issues, and it is not clear which issue it was decided on, issue preclusion cannot be used to prohibit a suit that will raise one of the two issues. Estoppel by judgment [a/k/a claim preclusion] precludes re-litigation of a cause of action finally determined between the parties and decrees that the judgment is rendered as a complete bar to any subsequent action on the same claim or cause of action. Plaintiff's cause of action here is a different cause of action from the one he litigated in the former case; therefore, estoppel by judgment does not apply. However, while we have just stated that claim preclusion does not apply in this case, issue preclusion [a/k/a/ estoppel by verdict] does. Here, plaintiff's two causes of action [comparing this suit and his former action] are not the same, but if the case at bar were to go to trial on all the issues raised in the pleadings and answer, some facts or questions determined and adjudicated in the earlier case would again be put in issue in this subsequent suit between the same parties. To protect the integrity of the prior judgment by precluding the possibility of opposite results by two different juries on the same set of facts, the doctrine of issue preclusion allows the judgment in the prior action to operate as an estoppel as to those facts or questions actually litigated and determined by the prior action. The problem at hand, then, is to determine what facts or questions were actually litigated in the prior case. We agree with the three concessions made by the defendant as to the effect of the verdict in the prior case, and specifically focus on the third: that because the prior case established that the defendant was negligent in order for the jury to have returned a verdict against plaintiff it had to have decided that he either sustained no damages or that his own negligence was a proximate cause of his damages. This third preposition places upon defendant the heavy burden outlined by

Illinois Central Railroad v. Parks

390 N.E.2d 1078 (1979)

Judge Shake in *Flora v, Indiana Service Co.*: "[W]here a judgment may have been based upon either or any of two or more distinct facts, a party desiring to plead the judgment as an estoppel by verdict or finding upon the particular fact involved in a subsequent suit must show that it went upon that fact, or else the question will be open to a new contention. The estoppel of a judgment is only presumptively conclusive, when it appears that the judgment could not have been rendered without deciding the particular matter brought in question. It is necessary to look to the complete record to ascertain what was the question in issue." Defendant argues that, because plaintiff's evidence as to his loss was uncontroverted, the jury's verdict had to be based upon a finding of contributory negligence. We are not convinced. We reviewed the complete record in the companion case and hold that the jury verdict against plaintiff in that case could mean that he had failed in his burden of proving compensable damages. We hold that defendant has failed its burden of showing that the judgment against plaintiff in the prior action could not have been rendered without deciding that he was contributorily negligent in the accident which precipitated the two lawsuits. Consequently, the trial court was correct in granting partial summary judgment estopping the railroad from denying its negligence and in limiting the issues at trial to whether Park (P) was contributorily negligent, whether any such contributory negligence was a proximate cause of the accident, and whether plaintiff sustained personal injuries and compensable damages.

C

Affirmed.

Parklane Hosiery Co. v. Shore

U.S. Supreme Court, 439 U.S. 322 (1979)

FACTS

A stockholder brought a class action suit against a company alleging the company issued a materially false and misleading proxy statement in connection with a merger. Shore (plaintiff), a stockholder, sued Parklane (defendant) alleging various causes of action in connection with a merger. The SEC filed suit against the defendant based on the same allegations as Shore but before Shore's case reached trial. The District Court ruled in favor of the SEC and entered a declaratory judgment and the Court of Appeals for the Second Circuit affirmed. Thereafter, Shore motioned for summary judgment claiming Parklane was collaterally estopped from litigating the same issues resolved in the SEC suit. The District Court denied the motion holding that estoppel would bar Parklane its Seventh Amendment Right to a jury trial. The Court of Appeals for the Second Circuit reversed and the Supreme Court of the United States granted certiorari.

I

(1) Where a court has determined that a party has had a full and fair opportunity to litigate facts, can that party be barred from re-litigating those same facts resolved adversely against it in prior equitable proceeding? (2) Is a party's 7th Amendment right to a jury trial violated via the use of offensive collateral estoppel?

R

Even in cases where the defendant will be dispossessed of the right to a jury trial, trial courts have broad discretion to apply the doctrine of offensive collateral estoppel.

A

Where a court has determined that a party has had a full and fair opportunity to litigate the facts in the prior equitable proceeding, that party will be barred from re-litigating those same facts which were resolved (adversely) against it, in a subsequent court of law. Thus, a trial judge should not allow the plaintiff to use offensive collateral estoppel where he could have easily joined the earlier action or where its application would be unfair and unjust to the defendant. In the instant case, the plaintiff should be allowed to use offensive collateral estoppel because he most likely could <u>not</u> have joined in the injunctive action brought by the SEC. Moreover, its application would not be unfair to Parklane because Parklane had every incentive to litigate the SEC lawsuit fully and vigorously in light of the severity of the charges against it and the anticipated litany of private lawsuits which might follow. A party's 7th Amendment right to a jury trial is not offended through the use of offensive collateral. The defendant argues that a 1791 historical interpretation should determine the extent of the 7th Amendment. That is, historically the common law has permitted collateral estoppel only where there was mutuality. But we fail see why the meaning of the 7th Amendment should depend on the existence of mutuality. A party is equally denied a jury trial when he is estopped from re-litigating the same facts/issues against the same/different party after losing in an equity suit; and collateral did not exist in 1791.

Parklane Hosiery Co. v. Shore

U.S. Supreme Court, 439 U.S. 322 (1979)

C Even in cases where the defendant will be dispossessed of the right to a jury trial, trial courts have broad discretion to apply the doctrine of offensive collateral estoppel.

State Farm Fire & Cas. Co. v. Century Home Components

550 P.2d 1185 (1976)

FACTS

Plaintiff State Farm stored some of its property in a warehouse about sixty feet from defendant Century Home's shed. The warehouse was connected to the shed by a wooden loading dock. On a Sunday morning in the summer of 1968, a fire started in the shed, eventually spreading to and destroying plaintiff's warehouse. The cause of the fire was disputed, but might have been caused by the defendant's janitor. Eventually, more than 50 lawsuits were filed against defendant for losses attributable to the fire. In the first three, two resulted in judgment for the plaintiffs and one resulted in a judgment for Century Home. Thus, defendant's negligence has been tried four times and three final judgments have been rendered. Defendant has procured one favorable judgment and the claimants have received two judgments. Following the entry of judgment in *Pacific N. W. Bell and Hesse*, plaintiff and a number of other plaintiffs filed amended complaints to match those cases, and asserted that the judgments therein should preclude defendant from again litigating the question of liability. Defendant, however, relied on the verdict in *Sylwester v. Century Home Components Inc.* to argue that it was not negligent and should not have to re-litigate negligence.

I

Can a court refuse to apply collateral estoppel in a subsequent suit when prior cases produce inconsistent verdicts?

R

Collateral estoppel would work an injustice where, in a prior case, there are existing determinations that are inconsistent on the matter in issue with those made in a subsequent case.

A

We believe that if the circumstances are such that our confidence in the integrity of the determination is severely undermined, or that the result would likely be different in a second trial, it would work an injustice to deny the litigant another chance. Thus, where it is apparent that the verdict was the result of a jury compromise, the losing party should not be precluded by the judgment. It has also been held that if the prior determination was manifestly erroneous the judgment should not be given preclusive effect. And the existence of newly discovered or crucial evidence that was not available to the litigant at the first trial would provide a basis for denying preclusion where it appears the evidence would have a significant effect on the outcome. We also agree with the commentators to the extent that, where outstanding determinations are actually inconsistent on the matter sought to be precluded, it would be patently unfair to estop a party by the judgment it lost. Thus, where there are extant determinations that are inconsistent on the matter in issue, that the application of collateral estoppel would likely work an injustice. There seems to be something fundamentally offensive about depriving a party of the opportunity to litigate the issue again when he has shown beyond a doubt that on another day he prevailed. The thrust of plaintiff's argument is that the determinations are not inconsistent because the issues in *Hesse and Pacific N.W. Bell* were not identical with the issues in *Sylwester*. It is true that the phrasing of the allegations of negligence differed and that certain specifications of negligence were not submitted to the jury in *Sylwester*. We do not give much weight to variations in the working of the pleadings, however, where essentially the same acts and omissions are alleged. The thrust of plaintiff's argument must be that the jury in *Hesse* and the court in *Pacific N.W. Bell* adjudicated defendant negligent in respects which were not considered by the jury in *Sylwester*. The records of these cases, however, do not permit such a conclusion. Since the jury in *Hesse* returned a general verdict, we do not know in which respects it found defendant negligent and, given the similarity of some of the allegations and the basic thrust of negligence alleged, we are unable to conclude that it found defendant negligent en the basis of conduct not submitted to the jury in *Sylwester*. We thus conclude that the prior determinations are basically inconsistent and that the circumstances are such that it would be unfair to preclude defendant from re-litigating the issue of liability.

Reversed.

Kovach v. District of Columbia

805 A.2d 957 (D.C. Ct. App. 2002)

FACTS

Plaintiff Donald Kovach was among 20,000 motorists who had been issued traffic tickets for running red lights. Many accidentally ran the light, as the camera designed to catch them running the light itself had an automatic red light that confused motorists. The District (Defendant) agreed to dismiss outstanding fines assessed to approximately 2,000 motorists whose infractions were recorded by the camera, but determined that those who had already paid would not be reimbursed. Kovach was among those who had paid the fine. He had paid it approximately five months before the District (D) decided to remove the camera. He filed suit against the District (D), arguing that the District's (D) decision to forgive some fines and enforce others was facially discriminatory under D.C. statutes and violated the Fifth and Fourteenth Amendments of the Constitution. The trial court ruled that his previous payment of a traffic violation precluded him from contesting the District's (D) subsequent decision to forgive only unpaid fines for violations recorded by the camera.

I Does admission of the commission of a violation in an administrative case preclude the re-litigation of issues involving the same parties and the same facts, not only as to every ground of recovery or defense actually presented in the action, but also as to every ground which might have been presented?

R Admission of the commission of a violation in an administrative case preclude the re-litigation of issues involving the same parties and the same facts, not only as to every ground of recovery or defense actually presented in the action, but also as to every ground that might have been presented.

A Yes. Admission of the commission of a violation in an administrative case preclude the re-litigation of issues involving the same parties and the same facts, not only as to every ground of recovery or defense actually presented in the action, but also as to every ground which might have been presented. The District (D) considers payment of a fine for a traffic violation admission of the commission of the infraction, and those who wish to contest a notice of infraction may do so before a hearing examiner of the Bureau of Traffic Adjudication (BTA), and, if appropriate, to an Appeals Board. However, the arguments in Kovach's (P) complaint, based on statutory and constitutional challenges, are distinct from the prior proceeding before the BTA. And the decision that Kovach (D) is challenging occurred five months after BTA's adjudication, and could not possibly have been raised before the BTA at the time when it adjudicated the traffic ticket. Therefore, res judicata does not bar Kovach's (D) claims. But the trial court's dismissal is nevertheless affirmed because collateral estoppel precludes Kovach (P) from challenging the District's (D) decision as discriminatory as applied to him. Even where res judicata--claim preclusion--is inapplicable, collateral estoppel--issue preclusion--may bar re-litigation of the issues settled in a prior action. Kovach (P) had the opportunity to contest the infraction before the BTA but did not.

C

Affirmed.

Durfee v. Duke

U.S. Supreme Court, 375 U.S. 106 (1963)

FACTS

Petitioners sued respondent in a Nebraska State Court to quiet title to certain land on the Missouri River, which is the boundary between Nebraska and Missouri. The Nebraska Court had jurisdiction over the subject matter only if the land was in Nebraska, and that depended on whether a shift in the river's course had been caused by avulsion or accretion. Respondent appeared in the Nebraska Court and fully litigated the issues, including that as to the Court's jurisdiction over the subject matter. The Court found in favor of petitioners and ordered that title to the land be quieted in them. The Nebraska Supreme Court affirmed, finding specifically that the rule of avulsion was applicable, that the land was in Nebraska, that the Nebraska courts had jurisdiction over the subject matter and that title to the land was in petitioners. Subsequently, respondent sued in a Missouri State Court to quiet title to the same land, claiming that it was in Missouri. The case was removed to a Federal District Court.

I

Must a court give full faith and credit to a judgment res judicata which has been fully and fairly litigated in another court?

R

A judgment is entitled to full faith and credit - even as to questions of jurisdiction - when the second court's inquiry discloses that those questions have been fully and fairly litigated and finally decided in the court which rendered the original judgment..

A

The judgment of the Nebraska Supreme Court was res judicata as to all issues, including the issue of jurisdiction, and it was binding on the District Court under the Full Faith and Credit Clause of the Constitution and the federal statute enacted to implement it. The constitutional command of full faith and credit, as implemented by Congress, requires that "judicial proceedings . . . shall have the same full faith and credit in every court within the United States . . . as they have by law or usage in the courts of such State . . . from which they are taken." Full faith and credit thus generally requires every State to give to a judgment at least the res judicata effect which the judgment would be accorded in the State which rendered it. "By the Constitutional provision for full faith and credit, the local doctrines of res judicata, speaking generally, become a part of national jurisprudence, and therefore federal questions cognizable here." *Riley v. New York Trust Co.* It is not questioned that the Nebraska courts would give full res judicata effect to the Nebraska judgment quieting title in the petitioners. It is the respondent's position, however, that whatever effect the Nebraska courts might give to the Nebraska judgment, the federal court in Missouri was free independently to determine whether the Nebraska court in fact had jurisdiction over the subject matter, i.e., whether the land in question was actually in Nebraska. In support of this position the respondent relies upon the many decisions of this Court which have held that a judgment of a court in one State is conclusive upon the merits in a court in another State only if the court in the first State had power to pass on the merits - had jurisdiction, that is, to render the judgment. As Mr. Justice Bradley stated the doctrine in the leading case of Thompson v. Whitman, "we think it clear that the jurisdiction of the court by which a judgment is rendered in any State may be questioned in a collateral proceeding in another State, notwithstanding the provision of the fourth article of the Constitution and the law of 1790, and notwithstanding the averments contained in the record of the judgment itself." The principle has been restated and applied in a variety of contexts. However, while it is established that a court in one State, when asked to give effect to the judgment of a court in another State, may constitutionally inquire into the foreign court's jurisdiction to render that judgment, the modern decisions of this Court have carefully delineated the permissible scope of such an inquiry. From these decisions there emerges the general rule that a judgment is entitled to full faith and credit - even as to questions of jurisdiction - when the second court's inquiry discloses that those questions have been fully and fairly litigated and finally decided in the court which rendered the original judgment. For the reasons stated, we hold in this case that the federal court in Missouri had the power and, upon proper averments, the duty to inquire into the jurisdiction of the Nebraska courts to render the decree quieting title to the land in the petitioners. We further hold that when that inquiry disclosed, as it did, that the jurisdictional issues had been fully and fairly litigated by the parties and finally determined in the Nebraska courts, the federal court in Missouri was correct in ruling that further inquiry was precluded. Accordingly the judgment of the Court of Appeals is reversed, and that of the District Court is affirmed.

C

Reversed.

United States v. Beggerly

U.S. Supreme Court, 524 U.S. 38 (1988)

FACTS

In 1979, the United States sued respondents and others to quiet title to land it sought for a federal park, contending that respondents did not have clear title because the Government had never patented the disputed land after acquiring it as part of the Louisiana Purchase. Government officials searched public land records during discovery, but reported to respondents that they found no proof of a grant to a private landowner. A 1982 settlement agreement quieted title in the Government's favor in return for a payment to respondents. In 1994, respondents sued to set aside the settlement agreement and obtain damages, claiming that they had evidence showing that the land had been granted to a private owner before the Louisiana Purchase, but the District Court concluded that it had no jurisdiction to hear the case. The Fifth Circuit reversed, finding two jurisdictional bases: (1) the suit was an "independent action" to set aside the settlement under Federal Rule of Civil Procedure 60(b); and (2) the Quiet Title Act (QTA or Act). In reaching the second conclusion, the court found that the QTA's 12-year statute of limitations was subject to equitable tolling and therefore suit was not barred by the fact that respondents had known about the Government's claim since 1979. The court then vacated the settlement agreement and instructed the District Court to quiet title in respondents' favor.

I

Can litigation res judicata be reopened when new evidence is uncovered?

R

Post-judgment relief may be obtained when the requirements for meritorious "independent action" have been met and such action should be available only to prevent a grave miscarriage of justice.

A

The Fifth Circuit had no jurisdiction over respondents' suit. Rule 60(b)'s history and language are inconsistent with the Government's position that an "independent action" to set aside a judgment requires an independent source of jurisdiction. The original Rule 60(b) established a new system to govern requests to reopen judgments. Because it was unclear whether that Rule provided the exclusive means for obtaining post-judgment relief, the Rule was amended in 1946 to clarify that nearly all of the old forms of obtaining relief from a judgment were abolished but that the "independent action" survived. However, this does not mean that the requirements for a meritorious independent action have been met here. Such actions should be available only to prevent a grave miscarriage of justice. Respondents' allegation that the United States failed to thoroughly search its records and make full disclosure to the District Court regarding the land grant obviously does not approach this demanding standard. Equitable tolling is not available in a QTA suit. Such tolling is not permissible where it is inconsistent with the relevant statute's text. The QTA's express 12-year statute of limitations runs from the date the plaintiff or his predecessor in interest "knew or should have known" of the United States' claim. Thus, the Act has already effectively allowed for equitable tolling. Given this fact and the QTA's unusually generous limitations period, extension of the statutory period would be unwarranted.

C

Reversed and remanded.

Plant v. Blazer Financial Services

598 F.2d 1357 (5th Cir. 1979)

FACTS

Plaintiff Theresa Plant executed a note in favor of defendant Blazer Financial Services, Inc. for $2,520 to be paid in monthly installments of $105. No payments were made on the note. Eight months later, plaintiff commenced a civil action under §1640 of the Truth-in-Lending Act for failure to make disclosures required by the Act. Defendant counterclaimed on the note for the unpaid balance. Based on defendant's failure to disclose a limitation on an after-acquired security interest, the trial court held the disclosures inadequate and awarded plaintiff the statutory penalty of $944.76 and $700 in attorney's fees. Defendant appealed this ruling.

I

Is an action on an underlying debt in default a compulsory counterclaim?

R

An action on an underlying debt in default is a compulsory counterclaim that must be asserted in a suit by the debtor on a truth-in-lending cause of action.

A

Plaintiff Plant challenges the trial court's ruling that defendant's counterclaim on the underlying debt was compulsory. The issue of whether a state debt counterclaim in a truth-in-lending action is compulsory or permissive is one of first impression in this Circuit, has never, to our knowledge, been decided by a court of appeals, and has received diverse treatment from a great number of district courts. Rule 13(a), Federal Rules of Civil Procedure, provides that a counterclaim is compulsory if it "arises out of the transaction or occurrence" that is the subject matter of the plaintiff's claim. Four tests have been suggested to further define when a claim and counterclaim arise from the same transaction. Of the four, the test which has commended itself to most courts, including our own, is the "logical relation test." This test is a loose standard which permits "a broad realistic interpretation in the interest of avoiding a multiplicity of suits." The hallmark of this approach is its flexibility. Applying the logical relationship test literally to the counterclaim in this case suggests its compulsory character because a single aggregate of operative facts, the loan transaction, gave rise to both parties' claims. Because a tallying of the results from the district courts which have decided this question, however, shows that a greater number have found such a counterclaim merely permissive, we subject the relationship between the claims to further analysis. The purpose of the Truth-in-Lending Act is to assure a meaningful disclosure of credit terms so that the consumer will be able to compare more readily the various credit terms available to him and avoid the uninformed use of credit. After careful consideration of the factors relied upon to find counterclaims permissive, we opt for the analysis applied by courts in several states in determining debt counterclaims to be compulsory. Consequently, to permit the debtor to recover from the creditor without taking the original loan into account would be a serious departure from the evenhanded treatment afforded both parties under the Act. Truth-in-lending claims can be brought in either state or federal court. To the extent this dual jurisdiction was intended to permit litigation of truth-in-lending claims in actions on the debt, it reflects a purpose that the debt claim and the truth-in-lending claims be handled together. We conclude that the obvious interrelationship of the claims and rights of the parties, coupled with the common factual basis of the claims, demonstrates a logical relationship between the claim and counterclaim under the logical relation test.

C

We affirm the trial court's determination that the debt counterclaim is compulsory.

Mosley v. General Motors Corp.

497 F.2d 1330 (8th Cir. 1974)

FACTS

Plaintiff Nathaniel Mosely and nine others joined in bringing this action individually and as class representatives alleging that their rights guaranteed under 42 U.S.C. Sec. 2000 et seq. and 42 U.S.C. Sec. 1981 were denied by defendant General Motors and the local Union by reason of their color and race. Each of the ten had, prior to the filing of the complaint, filed a charge with the Equal Employment Opportunity Commission (EEOC) asserting the facts underlying these claims. Pursuant thereto, the EEOC made a reasonable cause finding that GM and the Union had engaged in unlawful employment practices in violation of Title VII of the Civil Rights Act of 1964. All of the individual plaintiffs requested injunctive relief, back pay, attorneys' fees and costs. The class counts of the complaint also sought declaratory and injunctive relief, back pay, attorneys' fees and costs. The district court ordered that "insofar as the first ten counts are concerned, those ten counts shall be severed into ten separate causes of action," and each plaintiff was directed to bring a separate action based upon his complaint, duly and separately filed. Upon entering the order, and upon application of the plaintiffs, the district court found that its decision involved a controlling question of law as to which there is a substantial ground for difference of opinion and that any of the parties might make application for appeal under 28 U.S.C. §1292(b). The 8th Circuit granted the application to permit this interlocutory appeal.

I

Are the issues of ten plaintiffs sufficient to sustain joinder under Rule 20(a)?

R

The difficulties in ultimately adjudicating damages to various plaintiffs in a class are not so overwhelming as to require severance of the plaintiffs' causes of action and, if appropriate, separate trials may be granted as to any particular issue after a determination of common questions.

A

The issues of ten plaintiffs are sufficient to sustain joinder under Rule 20(a). The U.S. Supreme Court has said that under the Rules, the impulse is toward entertaining the broadest possible scope of action consistent with fairness to the parties. Thus, joinder of claims, parties and remedies is strongly encouraged but is not applicable to all cases. Rule 20(a) requires that a right to relief must be asserted by, or against, each plaintiff or defendant relating to or arising out of the same transaction or occurrence, or series of transactions or occurrences [i.e., the first requisite of joinder] ***and*** some question of law or fact common to all the parties must arise in the action [i.e., the second requisite of joinder]. In this case, plaintiff and the others have asserted a right to relief arising out of the same transactions or occurrences. Each of the ten plaintiffs alleged that he had been injured by the same general policy of discrimination on the part of GM and the Union. We conclude that a company-wide policy purportedly designed to discriminate against blacks in employment similarly arises out of the same series of transactions or occurrences.

Mosley v. General Motors Corp.

497 F.2d 1330 (8th Cir. 1974)

Therefore the plaintiff and the others meet the first requisite for joinder under Rule 20(a). The second requisite necessary to sustain a permissive joinder under the rule is that a question of law or fact common to all the parties will arise in the action. The rule does not require that ***all*** questions of law and fact raised by the dispute be common. The right to relief here depends on the ability to demonstrate that each of the plaintiffs was wronged by racially discriminatory policies on the part of GM and the Union. The discriminatory character of GM's and the Union's conduct is thus basic to each plaintiff's recovery. The fact that each plaintiff may have different effects from the alleged discrimination is immaterial for the purposes of determining the common question of law or fact. Thus we conclude that the second requisite for joinder under Rule 20(a) is also met by the complaint. For the reasons set forth above, we conclude that the district court abused its discretion in severing the joined actions. The judgment of the district court disallowing joinder of the plaintiffs' individual actions is reversed and remanded with directions to permit plaintiff and the other plaintiffs to proceed jointly.

C

See above.

Price v. CTB Inc.

U.S. District Court, 168 F.Supp.2d 1299 (M.D. Ala. 2001)

FACTS

Plaintiff Price, a chicken farmer, sued defendants CTB, Inc., a company in the business of equipping poultry houses, and Latco, a builder of chicken houses, for breach of contract, fraudulent misrepresentation, negligence, and wantonness in connection with the construction of a chicken house constructed by Latco. Six months after the complaint was filed, Latco moved to file a third-party complaint against defendant ITW, a nail manufacturer which allegedly negligently designed the nails used to construct the chicken house, seeking indemnity. ITW moved to dismiss for improper impleader.

I

Was third party defendant ITW properly impleaded into the action?

R

Under Rule 14(a), a defendant may assert a claim against anyone not a party to the original action if that third party's liability is in some way dependent upon the outcome of the original action.

A

Under Rule 14(a), "a defendant may assert a claim against anyone not a party to the original action if that third party's liability is in some way dependent upon the outcome of the original action." However, the third-party claim may not be based on a separate and independent claim, even though both claims share common underlying facts. Impleader is proper only when a defendant asserts that the liability for the original action is properly placed upon the third party. Alabama law does not recognize a right of contribution among joint tortfeasors. However, we do recognize implied contractual indemnity running from a manufacturer to a seller of its products. Under this doctrine, a manufacturer is bound to indemnify the seller if the seller is "without fault." Accordingly, defendant ITW has been properly impleaded into the action, since defendant Latco may have a right of indemnity against ITW.

C

Motion denied.

Kroger v. Omaha Public Power District

523 F.2d 161 (8th Cir. 1975)

FACTS

James Kroger was employed by Paxton & Vierling Steel Company at its factory in Carter Lake, Iowa. While walking alongside a large steel tank being moved by crane, James was killed when the boom of the crane came close enough to high-tension lines that electricity from those lines arced over to the boom, then to the tank and then over to James, killing him. Defendant-appellee Omaha Public Power District (OPPD), a public corporation of the state of Nebraska, had at one time owned the transmission lines involved. However, six years prior to the fatal accident, OPPD sold the lines and equipment to Paxton & Vierling. A relationship between the two companies still existed: OPPD thereafter sold electricity to Paxton & Vierling, and when so requested, made repairs upon the lines and equipment. Plaintiff-appellant Geraldine Kroger, the administratrix of the estate of the deceased, brought a wrongful death suit based on diversity jurisdiction. The district court found that OPPD owed no duty to James, and granted its motion for summary judgment.

I

Does OPPD owe a duty to James Kroger, the breach of which would give rise to liability?

R

If the court concludes that, as a matter of law, the defendant owed no duty, summary judgment may be granted.

A

The District Court properly based its order of summary judgment on the fact that (1) Paxton & Vierling undeniably owned the transmission lines at the time of the accident; (2) OPPD had no duty to maintain such lines; (3) OPPD had not been requested to discontinue the flow of electricity on the date of the accident; and (4) OPPD had not been put on notice that a crane was being operated in the vicinity of the lines. As a result, there was no duty owed by OPPD to James Kroger, the breach of which would give rise to liability. We agree with the findings of the District Court and thus affirm the order of summary judgment.

C

See above.

Owen Equipment & Erection Co. v. Kroger

U.S. Supreme Court, 437 U.S. 365 (1978)

FACTS

Plaintiff Mrs. Kroger brought a wrongful death suit against Defendant Omaha Public Power District (OPPD) when the plaintiff's husband was electrocuted while walking too close to a metal crane which was in close proximity to high tension lines operated by OPPD. The plaintiff was a citizen of Iowa and OPPD was a Nebraska corporation. The plaintiff brought suit in federal court based diversity of citizenship. OPPD then filed a third-party complaint against Owen Equipment & Erection Co. (Owen) alleging that Owen's negligence proximately caused the death of the plaintiff's husband. Kroger thereafter amended her complaint to include Defendant Owen. However, Defendant Owen's principle place of business was actually Iowa and OPPD was granted Summary Judgment as diversity was lacking. Defendant Owen then moved to dismiss based on lack of subject matter jurisdiction. The District Court denied the motion and the Court of Appeals affirmed. The Supreme Court of the United States granted certiorari.

I

When a plaintiff adds another party (a pendent party) who destroys complete diversity, does a federal court still retain jurisdiction based on diversity?

R

When a plaintiff adds a pendent party who destroys complete diversity, Federal Courts do not retain jurisdiction based on diversity.

A

Congress has always required complete diversity of citizenship in cases such as these. Therefore, no plaintiff may be a citizen of the same state as any defendant. The plaintiff could not have originally brought suit against both Defendant Owen and Defendant OPPD based on diversity. Thus, the plaintiff should not be allowed to obtain federal diversity jurisdiction by naming only the diverse party, OPPD, in her original suit and waiting for Defendant OPPD to implead the non-diverse party, Owen. This, if allowed, would permit plaintiffs to circumvent the diversity requirements of §1332(a)(1).

C

No. The Federal Courts do not retain jurisdiction based on diversity when the plaintiff adds a pendent party who destroys complete diversity.

Temple v. Synthes Corp.

U.S. Supreme Court, 498 U.S. 1092 (1990)

FACTS

Plaintiff Temple underwent surgery in which a synthetic medical device (a plate) manufactured by Defendant Synthes Corp. was placed in his back. The screws of the device broke after surgery and the plaintiff sued. The plaintiff sued his doctor, the hospital and the medical device manufacturer (Synthes Corp.) in separate proceedings for the injuries he sustained as a result of the implanted device. He instituted both a federal cause of action and a state cause of action. Plaintiff sued the device manufacturer in Louisiana federal court on diversity grounds alleging various design and manufacturing defects and brought a separate state administrative action against the doctor and the hospital. At the conclusion the hearing, the plaintiff sued the doctor and the hospital in Louisiana state court. The defendant (Synthes) filed a motion to dismiss arguing that both the doctor and the hospital should have been joined in one suit. The District Court ordered the joinder but the plaintiff refused to comply and the District Court dismissed the action with prejudice. The Fifth Circuit Court of Appeals affirmed the dismissal and the United States Supreme Court granted certiorari.

I

Must all interested parties be joined in (made a party to) the same lawsuit?

R

It is not always necessary to join all interested parties in the same lawsuit.

A

This case focuses on the importance of joinder, as governed by Rule 19 of the Federal Rules of Civil Procedure. It states that a party must be joined in a lawsuit if complete relief cannot be granted without that party. The doctor and hospital were permissive parties, whose joinder was not required. The court agreed with Plaintiff Temple that it was an error to label the joint tortfeasors as indispensable parties and therefore dismissed the lawsuit under Rule 19(b). Rule 19(b) states that a court may dismiss a suit if such joinder is not possible.

C

No. It is not always necessary to join all interested parties in the same lawsuit. Reversed and remanded.

Helzberg's Diamond Shops v. Valley West Des Moines

564 F.2d 816 (8th Cir. 1977)

FACTS

On February 3, 1975, plaintiff Helzberg's Diamond Shops, Inc. and defendant Valley West Des Moines Shopping Center entered into a written lease agreement which granted plaintiff the right to operate a full line jewelry store. Section 6 of Article V of the lease agreement provided that defendant "agrees it will not lease premises in the shopping center for use as a catalog jewelry store nor lease premises for more than two full line jewelry stores in the shopping center in addition to the leased premises." Thereafter, plaintiff commenced operation of a full-time jewelry store in the Valley West Mall. During the next twenty one months, defendant and two other corporations entered into leases for spaces in the Valley West Mall for use as full line jewelry stores. Pursuant to those leases, the two corporations also initiated actual operation of full line jewelry stores. On November 2, 1976, defendant and Kirk's Incorporated, doing business as Lord's Jewelers, entered into a written lease agreement granting Lord's the right to occupy space in Valley West Mall "only as a retail specialty jewelry store (and not as a catalogue or full line jewelry store)." However, Lord's intended to open and operate what constituted a full line jewelry store at space 261. In an attempt to avoid the opening of a fourth full line jewelry store in the Valley West Mall and the resulting breach of the Helzberg-Valley West (plaintiff-defendant) lease agreement, plaintiff instituted suit seeking preliminary and permanent injunctive relief restraining defendant's breach of the lease agreement. The suit was filed in the United States District Court for the Western District of Missouri. Subject matter jurisdiction was invoked pursuant to 28 U.S.C. §1332 based upon diversity of citizenship between the parties and an amount in controversy which exceeded the statutory amount. Personal jurisdiction was established by service of process on defendant pursuant to the Missouri "long arm" statute. Defendant moved to dismiss pursuant to Rule 19 because plaintiff had failed to join Lord's as a party defendant. The motion was denied. The district court went on to order (in relevant part) that pending the determination of the action on the merits, defendant is enjoined and restrained from allowing, and shall take all necessary steps to prevent, any other tenant in its Valley West Mall (including but not limited to Lord's Jewelers) to open and operate a fourth full line jewelry store. From this order, defendant appealed.

I

Did the district court erroneously deny defendant Valley West's motion to dismiss for failure to join an indispensable party?

R

Generally, a person does not become indispensable to an action simply because that person's rights or obligations under an entirely separate contract will be affected by the result of the action

A

After considering the factors which Rule 19(b) mandates be considered, the District Court concluded that Lord's was not to be regarded as indispensable. We agree. Lord's absence will not prejudice defendant

Valley West in a way contemplated by Rule 19(b). Defendant Valley West contends that it may be subjected to inconsistent obligations as a result of a determination in this action and a determination in another forum that defendant Valley West should proceed in a fashion contrary to what has been ordered in these proceedings. It is true that the obligations of defendant Valley West to plaintiff Helzberg, as determined in these proceedings, may be inconsistent with defendant Valley West's obligations to Lord's. However, we are of the opinion that any inconsistency in those obligations will result from defendant Valley West's voluntary execution of two lease agreements which impose inconsistent obligations rather than from Lord's absence from the present proceedings. Defendant Valley West's contention that it may be subjected to inconsistent judgments if Lord's should choose to file suit elsewhere and be awarded judgment is speculative at best. In the first place, Lord's has not filed such a suit. Secondly, there is no showing that another court is likely to interpret the language of the two lease agreements differently from the way in which the District Court would. Therefore, we also conclude that defendant Valley West will suffer no prejudice as a result of the District Court's proceeding in Lord's absence. Rule 19(b) also requires the court to consider ways in which prejudice to the absent party can be lessened or avoided. The District Court afforded Lord's the opportunity to intervene in order to protect any interest it might have in the outcome of this litigation. Lord's chose not to do so. Thus, we conclude that the district court properly denied the motion to dismiss for failure to join an indispensable party.

C The judgment of the District Court is affirmed.

National Resources Defense Council v. United States Nuclear Regulatory Commission

578 F.2d 1341 (10th Cir. 1978)

FACTS

The American Mining Congress and Kerr-McGee Nuclear Corporation seek review of the district court's order denying their motions to intervene as a matter of right or on a permissive basis, pursuant to Rule 24(a)(2) [applicant claims interest relating to the property or transaction, and disposition of the action may impair or impede ability to protect that interest, unless interests are adequately protected] and (b). The underlying action in which the movants requested intervention was instituted by the Natural Resources Defense Council (plaintiffs) and others. In the action, declaratory and injunctive relief is directed to the United States Nuclear Regulatory Commission (NRC) (defendant) and the New Mexico Environmental Improvement Agency (NMEIA), prohibiting those agencies from issuing licenses for the operation of uranium mills in New Mexico without first preparing environmental impact statements. Kerr-McGee and United Nuclear are potential recipients of the licenses. Congress, in the Atomic Energy Act of 1954, has authorized the NRC to issue such licenses. NMEIA is involved because under Sec. 274(b) of the Act, the NRC is authorized to enter into such agreements with the states allowing the states to issue licenses. Thus the action in effect seeks to prevent the use of Sec. 274(b) of the Act so as to avoid the requirement of an impact statement for which provision is made in the National Environmental Policy Act. The relief sought by the National Resources Defense Council's (plaintiff) complaint is, first, that NRC's involvement in the licensing procedure in New Mexico is, notwithstanding the delegation to the state, sufficient to constitute major federal action, whereby the impact statement requirement is not eliminated. Second, that if an impact statement is not required in connection with the granting of licenses, the New Mexico program is in conflict with Sec. 274(d)(2) of the Atomic Energy Act. The motion of United Nuclear Corporation to intervene was not opposed by the parties and it was granted. On the date the complaint was filed, NMEIA granted a license to United Nuclear to operate a uranium mill. The complaint seeks to enjoin the issuance of the license thus granted. It was after that, that Kerr-McGee, American Mining Congress, and others filed motions to intervene. These motions, insofar as they sought intervention as of right, were denied on the ground that the interests of the parties or movants would be adequately represented by United Nuclear. Permissive intervention was also denied. Kerr-McGee and American Mining Congress both appeal denial of both intervention as of right and permissive intervention.

I Was the Court's denial of intervention correct under Rule 24(a) of the Federal Rules of Civil Procedure?

R Applicants satisfying their burden of the three requirements of Rule 24(a)(2) should be allowed to intervene in an action.

National Resources Defense Council v. United States Nuclear Regulatory Commission

578 F.2d 1341 (10th Cir. 1978)

A

Our issue is a limited one. We merely construe and weigh Rule 24(a), intervention as of right, and decide in light of the facts and considerations presented whether the denial of intervention was correct. Accordingly, we must consider the standards set forth in subsection (2), which are: (1) whether the applicant claims an interest relating to the property or transaction which is the subject of the action; (2) whether the claimants are so situated that the disposition of the action may as a practical matter impair or impede their ability to protect that interest; and (3) whether their interest is not so adequately represented by existing parties. Strictly to require that the movant in intervention have a direct interest in the outcome of the lawsuit strikes us as being too narrow a construction of Rule 24(a)(2). A decision in favor of the Natural Resources Defense Council (P), which is not unlikely, could have a profound effect upon Kerr-McGee. Hence, it does have an interest within the meaning of Rule 24(a)(2). The next question is whether, assuming the existence of an interest, the chance of impairment is sufficient to fulfill the requirement of Rule 24(a)(2). The question of impairment is not separate from the question of existence of an interest. The Rule refers to impairment "as a practical matter," thus the court may consider any significant legal effect in Kerr-McGee's and the American Mining Congress' interest and is not restricted to a rigid res judicata test. Hence, the stare decisis effect might be sufficient to satisfy the requirement. We are of the opinion, therefore, that Kerr-McGee and the American Mining Congress have satisfied the impairment criterion. The final question is whether the trial court was correct in its conclusion that United Nuclear would adequately represent Kerr-McGee and the American Mining Congress. United Nuclear has already been granted its license, thus Kerr-McGee urges that United Nuclear may be ready to compromise the case by obtaining a mere declaration that while environmental impact statements should be issued, this requirement need be prospective only, whereby it would not affect them. While we see this as a remote possibility, we gravely doubt that United Nuclear would opt for such a result. However, there are other reasons for allowing intervention. There is some value in having the parties before the court so that they will be bound by the result and American Mining Congress represents a number of companies having a wide variety of interests. This can, therefore, provide a useful supplement to the defense of the case. The same can be said of Kerr-McGee. Thus Kerr-McGee and the American Mining Congress have satisfied their burden of the three requirements of Rule 24(A)(2). Consequently, they should be and they are hereby allowed to intervene. The order of the district court is reversed and the cause is remanded with instructions to the trial court to grant Kerr-McGee's and the American Mining Congress' motions to intervene.

C

See above.

Martin v. Wilks

U.S. Supreme Court, 490 U.S. 755 (1989)

FACTS

As the result of racial discrimination in hiring and promotion alleged by black firefighters against the City of Birmingham, the City of Birmingham (City) and the Jefferson County Personnel Board (Board) (defendants) entered into a consent judgment. Afterwards, the plaintiffs (white firefighters via "Martin"), sued the City and the Board alleging reverse discrimination in that the promotions of the black firefighters were in violation of federal law because they were based on race. Both the City and the Board defended arguing that the consent judgment barred the instant cause of action. The District Court agreed and held that the consent judgment was a defense to the reverse discrimination alleged by the white firefighters. The Court of Appeals reversed the District Court's decision holding that the consent judgment did not preclude the current suit because the white firefighters were not parties to the previous judgment. The U.S. Supreme Court granted certiorari.

I

Without forcibly joining a party (mandatory joinder) to the action, may another party seeking a judgment bind the former and obligate that party to intervene in the action?

R

One party seeking a judgment cannot bind another party and obligate that party to intervene in the action without the use of mandatory joinder.

A

One party seeking a judgment cannot bind another party and obligate that party to intervene in the action without the use of mandatory joinder. Both the City and the Board contend that the plaintiffs' suit is impermissible because the white firefighters failed to voluntarily intervene in the earlier action. This is highlighted by the fact that they knew that the consent judgment would affect them. However, we adopt the view in *Chase National Bank v. Norwalk*, where a person entitled to a hearing does not have the burden of voluntary intervention in a suit in which he is not a party. Thus, the method by which potential parties are subjected to the jurisdiction of the court and bound by judgment or decree is through the use of joinder of a party; not by mere knowledge of the existence of a lawsuit and not through the opportunity to intervene.

C

No. One party seeking a judgment cannot bind another party and obligate that party to intervene in the action without the use of mandatory joinder. Judgment affirmed.

Cohen v. The Republic of the Philippines

146 F.R.D. 90 (S.D.N.Y. 1993)

FACTS

This is an interpleader action initiated by Marc Cohen and Marc Cohen & Co. (collectively "Cohen") (plaintiffs) against Klaus Braemer and The Republic of the Philippines (defendant). The action is presently before the Court on the motion of Imelda R. Marcos for leave to intervene. At issue in this interpleader action is the ownership of four paintings whose total value is nearly $5 million. In late 1991 or 1992, Cohen received the paintings on consignment from Braemer, who was Marcos' agent entrusted to run her New York home in which the paintings had previously hung. Braemer demanded return of the paintings in March of 1992, but Cohen refused because he was uncertain who actually owned the paintings. Consequently, Cohen brought this interpleader action. Braemer claims that Marcos authorized him to sell the paintings, and he asserts a direct interest in the paintings originating from a loan he made to Marcos, the Philippines claims that the paintings were acquired with Government funds, or that the paintings were acquired with funds which Marcos or her husband illegally obtained. Either way, the Philippines claims to be the rightful owner of the paintings. Marcos now seeks to intervene in this action, claiming that the paintings were acquired with her personal funds and remain her property.

I

May a person intervene in an action if she has an interest relating to property which is the subject of the action?

R

Rule 24 allows ***anyone*** to intervene in a ***timely*** manner in an action if the applicant claims an interest relating to the property or transaction, and that interest is subject to possible prejudice and lack of adequate representation.

A

Rule 24 allows ***anyone*** to intervene in a ***timely*** manner in an action if the applicant claims an interest relating to the property or transaction, and that interest is subject to possible prejudice and lack of adequate representation. Marcos' application for intervention was made about five months after the initial complaint was filed. However, we believe Marcos' delay was not unreasonable given the complex and politically sensitive international implications of this action and further believe that the existing parties have not been unduly prejudiced by the delay. We do believe that Marcos' interest is very likely to be prejudiced if her intervention is denied. Her interest in the paintings is (1) sufficient to support her motion to intervene; (2) may be impaired by the action if she is not allowed to intervene; and (3) is not adequately protected by the existing parties. Marcos claims an interest in the paintings superior to that of the Government of the Philippines (plaintiff), and she disputes defendant Braemer's security therein. Thus, defendant can not adequately protect her interest.

C

Motion Marcos fulfills all the requirements of Rule 24(a)(2), and her motion to intervene is, therefore, granted.

Communities for Equity v. Michigan High School Athletic Assn.

1999 U.S. Dist. LEXIS 5780 (W.D. Mich. 1999)

FACTS

Plaintiff Communities for Equity bring this suit against defendant Michigan High School Athletic Association and its Representative Council, alleging that the former has been excluded from opportunities to participate in interscholastic athletic programs and have received unequal treatment and benefits in these programs. They contend that this putative exclusion and unequal treatment constitute gender discrimination, in violation of Title IX of the Education Amendments of 1972, the Equal Protection Clause of the Fourteenth Amendment; and Michigan State laws. The alleged discrimination is made manifest, according to plaintiff, in defendant's: (1) refusing to sanction girls' ice hockey and water polo; (2) requiring that the plaintiff's Class play its sports in non-traditional seasons; (3) operating shorter athletic seasons for some girls' sports than for boys' sports; (4) scheduling the competitions of plaintiff's Class on inferior dates; (5) providing, assigning, and operating inferior athletic facilities to the plaintiff's Class in which to play defendant-sanctioned games; (6) requiring that the plaintiff's Class play some sports under rules and/or conditions different from those in the NCAA or other governing organizations, unlike boys; and (7) allocating more resources for the support and promotion of male interscholastic athletic programs than for female programs. Plaintiff's motion for Class Certification asks the Court to define the proposed class as follows: all present and future female students enrolled in defendant's member schools who participate in interscholastic athletics or who are deterred from participating in interscholastic athletics because of defendant's discriminatory conduct and who are adversely affected by that conduct.

I

If a group of high school female athletes meet all the requirements of Rule 23, must class certification be granted?

R

A class is not maintainable merely because the complaint mimics Rule 23 requirements - a hearing may be necessary for the court to probe behind the pleadings before coming to rest on certification question.

A

According to the U.S. Supreme Court, this Court must conduct a "rigorous analysis" into whether the prerequisites of Rule 23 are met before certifying a class action. The "rigorous analysis" requirement means that a class is not maintainable merely because the complaint parrots the legal requirements of Rule 23. Although a hearing prior to the class determination is not always required, it may be necessary for the Court to probe behind the pleadings before coming to rest on the certification question. In this case, the extensive briefing filed by the parties, the Court's past review of motions, and the documentary evidence and affidavits filed make the hearing of evidence unnecessary because the Court is able to

Communities for Equity v. Michigan High School Athletic Assn.

1999 U.S. Dist. LEXIS 5780 (W.D. Mich. 1999)

probe behind the pleadings without additional evidence or argument. In this case, the numbers themselves justify a conclusion of numerosity and impracticability of joinder. Under Communities for Equity's theory of liability, thousands of female high school athletes and would-be athletes are subjected to Michigan High School Athletic Association's alleged discriminatory practices. We thus conclude that the numerosity requirement is satisfied by the proposed class. Next, the Rule requires commonality – that there are questions of law and fact common to class members. To the extent that the underlying issue in this case is one of unequal treatment and discrimination, the matter of whether to sanction a particular sport appears to be one relating to relief, rather than liability. The Court determines that the requirements are met. Michigan High School Athletic Association argues that a class is unnecessary, because relief granted to the named plaintiffs would inure to the benefit of the class. Even if such a requirement existed, mootness concerns would suggest the necessity of certification. Therefore, it is the conclusion of this Court that the motion for Class Certification shall be granted. The class action is certified as to the following class: all present and future female students enrolled in Michigan High School Athletic Association member schools who participate in interscholastic athletics or who are deterred from participating in interscholastic athletics because of Michigan High School Athletic Association's discriminatory conduct and who are adversely affected by that conduct.

C See above.

Heaven v. Trust Company Bank

U.S. Court of Appeals, 118 F.3d 735 (11th Cir. 1997)

FACTS

Plaintiff Ranae Heaven leased a Ford Taurus from defendant Sun Trust, signing a preprinted lease agreement provided by it. Later, plaintiff brought this action alleging that Sun Trust failed to comply with the strict disclosure requirements of the Consumer Leasing Act (CLA) and Regulation M (implementing the Act). Plaintiff sued for the statutory penalty and attorney fees but alleged no actual damages. She sought to certify a class pursuant to Rule 23(a) [class so numerous that joinder of all is impractical, common question of law or fact, claims and defenses of representatives are typical, representatives will fairly and adequately represent interests of class] and (b)(3) [common questions or law or fact predominate, class action is superior to other approaches; pertinent findings include the interest of members of class in individually controlling prosecution of separate actions, extent litigation already commenced, desirability of concentrating litigation, difficulties in managing the class]. Defendant counterclaimed on the alternative grounds that individual class members had defaulted on the terms of their lease agreements, and/or made false statements in their lease applications. The district court denied certification of the class.

I

Was the district court's denial of the motion to certify a class consistent with the requirements of Rule 23(b)(3) and facts and circumstances of the case?

R

There is no abuse of discretion in denying a class action as long as the district court has given due consideration to all the relevant factors of Rule 23 within the context of a "rigorous analysis" and has not made any impermissible inferences.

A

The district court concluded plaintiff had not established that her action met the requirements of subdivision (b)(3) for class certification. We agree with that assessment. First, the court determined that defendant counterclaims were compulsory under Rule 13(a). We agree. Plaintiff does not dispute that debt counterclaims are compulsory in TILA and CLA cases as a general matter. However, she contends that the presence of counterclaims cannot be a basis for denying class certification, relying on *Roper v. Consurve Inc*. We do not believe that *Roper* states such a general rule. The court below considered the nature of defendant's counterclaims and determined that individual lessee counterclaim defendants would be compelled to come forward with individual defenses. This would require the court to engage in multiple separate factual determinations. The court also determined that the interests of some individual class members in controlling their own case would be compromised. Their exposure as counterclaim defendants could well exceed the amount they might recover for statutory penalties as class members. The statutory claims asserted by the class would be against the interests of these individual class members. This is a proper factor to be considered under 13(a). Thus, where the district

---

court has given due consideration to all relevant factors within the context of a rigorous analysis and has not relied on impermissible factors, we are unable to find an abuse of discretion. If, after such an evaluation, the district court is convinced that a class action is not superior to other available methods for the fair and efficient adjudication of the controversy, we cannot second guess that conclusion under the applicable standard of review.

C Affirmed.

Hansberry v. Lee

U.S. Supreme Court, 11 U.S. 32 (1940)

FACTS

Plaintiff Lee, a white male, sought to enjoin the purchase of some restricted land by Defendant Hansberry, a black male. Plaintiff Lee alleged that the seller had signed a racially restrictive covenant and that an earlier state court decision held that the covenant was effective since 95% of the landowners had signed it. Defendant Hansberry and the other defendants argued that they were not bound by the *res judicata* effect of an earlier judgment, since they were not parties to the suit and because their due process rights were being violated. The Illinois Circuit Court and Supreme Court held that the original action was a class action suit and therefore its holding was binding on all class members including the defendants. The Supreme Court of the United States granted certiorari.

I

Is a judgment *res judicata* and therefore binding on absent parties where the procedural requirements for class action have not been satisfied?

R

Due process is violated when a class action judgment was given *res judicata* effect but when the prerequisites and procedures for the class action were not satisfied.

A

Due process is violated when a class action judgment was given *res judicata* effect but prerequisites and procedures for the class action were not satisfied. This is because to hold otherwise would violate the due process rights of the absent members. Notice and an opportunity to be heard are absolutely required for due process and a judgment in which a person is not designated a party can not have *res judicata* thrust upon him. In the instant case, where the lower court found the covenant effective, the procedure did not adequately protect the interests of the defendants. First, the restrictive agreement did not purport to create a joint obligation or liability. Rather, the racially restrictive covenant was a series of several obligations of the signers. Moreover, the parties seeking to enforce the agreement cannot be considered members of the same class as those parties seeking to challenge the validity of the agreement or to resist its performance. Thus, the mere fact that all of the parties had signed the agreement does not make them of the same class. Thus, the absent parties in the original litigation were not provided due process protections in asserting their interests.

C

No. Due process is violated when a class action judgment was given *res judicata* effect but when the prerequisites and procedures for the class action were not satisfied.

Philips Petroleum v. Shutts

U.S. Supreme Court, 472 U.S. 797 (1985)

FACTS

Various plaintiffs brought suit against the defendant to recover royalty payments owed. Defendant Phillips Petroleum obtained natural gas from leased land in eleven different states. Plaintiff Shutts and several other lessors brought an action against Defendant Phillips Petroleum to recover interest on royalty payments due under their leases. The Kansas trial court certified a class consisting of 33,000 royalty owners and the class representatives were provided notice by first class mail with an opportunity to respond. The final class consisted of 28,100 class members from all 50 states. The trial court, asserted personal jurisdiction and applied only Kansas contract law finding Phillips Petroleum liable for the interest due. Defendant Phillips Petroleum argued that the Due Process Clause prevented the Kansas court from adjudicating the claims of the non-resident class members and that the Full Faith and Credit Clause prohibited the application of Kansas law to all of the claims. The Kansas Supreme Court affirmed the trial court's holding and the Supreme Court of the United States granted certiorari.

I

(1) When a classes' absent members do not possess the minimum contacts with the forum which would support personal jurisdiction over them, may the court still exercise personal jurisdiction over them? (2) Are the notice requirements of due process satisfied by a mailed notice and opt out provision? (3) When the state does not have a significant contact and interest in every claim asserted by each member of the class, may a forum state apply that state's law to every claim in a class action?

R

The forum state must have sufficient interests in the claims to assert its state law to all of the claims; however, personal jurisdiction does not require that each class member have minimum contacts with the forum state in class action suits.

A

(1) Yes. When a classes' absent class members do not possess the minimum contacts with the forum which would support personal jurisdiction over a defendant, a court may exercise personal jurisdiction over them. Due Process requires that a defendant have sufficient minimum contacts with the forum state in order for a court to obtain personal jurisdiction over the defendant. However, there are significant differences between jurisdiction over a defendant and jurisdiction over a class of plaintiffs. While defendants deserve due process protections from being hauled into a distant state with which the defendants have no contacts, the plaintiffs in a class action are not hauled anywhere to defend themselves. In class actions, class representatives protect the interests of absent class members and those members need not hire counsel or appear. (2) Yes. The notice requirement for due process purposes are satisfied by a mailed notice with an "opt out" provision. The notice must be calculated to provide reasonable notice and apprise the parties of the pendency of the actions. In the instant case, the class representatives used first class mail to notify all 33,000 royalty owners of the pending action. (3) No. Where the state does not have a significant interest in every claim asserted by each

member of the class, a forum state may not apply that state's law to every claim in a class action. In the case at hand, the Kansas state court applied Kansas contract law to every claim, notwithstanding that over 99% of the leases and 97% of the plaintiffs had no apparent connection to Kansas. The defendant contends that the application of Kansas substantive law in this situation violates the Due Process Clause and the Full Faith and Credit Clause, and we agree.

C The forum state must have sufficient interests in the claims to assert its state law to all of the claims; however, personal jurisdiction does not require that each class member have minimum contacts with the forum state in class action suits.

Amchem Products Inc. v. Windsor

U.S. Supreme Court, 521 U.S. 591 (1997)

FACTS

Defendant Amchem and the other asbestos manufacturers filed a fraudulent lawsuit, which certified current and future plaintiffs as a class, for the purposes of making them accept a stipulated settlement. A District Court conditionally certified the class. Many of the plaintiff class members appealed, arguing that the settlement disadvantaged them unfairly because it did not adjust for inflation, did not account for changes in medical understanding, paid low compensation and did not compensate for certain claims. The Court of Appeals decertified the class finding: (1) individual cases predominated because class members were exposed to different asbestos products over different period of time and suffered from different symptoms; (2) the case law governing the members varied; (3) representation was inadequate due to serious intra class conflicts; and (4) the class action was not superior to individual suits, since it was so large and complex making adjudication of the suit nearly impossible. The other asbestos manufacturers appealed.

I

Must the requirements of Rule 23 be met by class action settlement offers?

R

Class action settlement offers must meet the Rule 23 requirements of: (1) predominance; (2) superiority; (3) adequate representation; and (4) notice before it can be certified.

A

Class action settlement offers must meet the Rule 23 requirements of: (1) predominance; (2) superiority; (3) adequate representation; and (4) notice before it can be certified. The District Court must consider Rule 23's requirements to protect absentee class members. Rule 23 requires a consideration as to whether a proposed class has sufficient utility such that the absent members can fairly be bound by the class representatives' decisions. Here the District Court found predominance based on the class members shared experience in asbestos exposure and in receiving fair and prompt compensation. However, these findings do not satisfy Rule 23(b)(3). The benefits asbestos victims may obtain from a grand scale compensation scheme is a matter for legislative consideration but irrelevant to the predominance inquiry. The Rule 23(b)(3) predominance inquiry tests whether proposed classes are sufficiently cohesive to warrant adjudication by representation. Here, the mere fact that all the plaintiffs were injured by asbestos does not mean the 23(b)(2) predominance requirement has been met.

C

Affirmed

NOTES

NOTES

NOTES

NOTES

NOTES

NOTES

NOTES

NOTES

NOTES

NOTES

NOTES

NOTES

NOTES

NOTES

NOTES

NOTES

McLaren Legal Publishers LLC

For a full catalog,

please visit our website at:

www.mclarenpublishing.com